# CLASSIC
# GEORGIAN STYLE

# CLASSIC
# GEORGIAN STYLE

## HENRIETTA SPENCER-CHURCHILL

RIZZOLI
NEW YORK

DEDICATION

*To Roy*

First published in the United States of America in 1997 by
Rizzoli International Publications, Inc.
300 Park Avenue South, New York, NY 10010

First published in Great Britain in 1997 by
Collins & Brown Limited

ISBN: 0-8478-2042-4
LC: 97-66475

Project editor: Alexandra Parsons
Designer: Christine Wood
Photography: Kim Sayer
Additional text: Philippa Lewis

Reproduction by Bright Arts Graphics
Printed and bound in Italy by L.E.G.O.

# CONTENTS

# ✦❧ INTRODUCTION ❧✦

WE ALL THINK we know what the perfect Georgian house should look like, but there is no one typical 'look'. There are as many variations on the theme as you would expect from an era that spanned nearly 120 years and witnessed significant upheavals in the social and economic life of Britain.

In terms of the visual arts and architecture of the Georgian period, the different styles can be loosely divided into four main artistic movements: Palladianism, rococo, neoclassicism and Regency. Within those stylistic developments there were many other popular themes based on new interpretations of revivals inspired by sources as diverse as Etruscan friezes and medieval cathedrals.

Although the Georgian style is synonymous with England in the 18th century, its influence was felt in other parts of Europe and in America, and it was not all one-way traffic. In France, for instance, the rococo style that flourished there in the first half of the century, subsequently inspired many mid-Georgian English interiors. In America, a particularly American form of Georgian style emerged that can be split into two main periods: Colonial, which mirrored the simple elegance of the early Georgian period and lasted until the Declaration of Independence in 1776, followed by Federal which incorporated both neoclassical and Regency styles.

The one theme that ran through the rigorous symmetry of the Palladians, the swags and ornament of the rococo period and the clean lines of the Regency style, was an unerring sense of style: proportions that pleased the eye and the landscape and a quality of craftsmanship that has rarely been bettered. Terraced town houses, simple country villas and grand mansions were built as a stylistic whole, with an impressive attention to detail. Gardens, landscaped parks and farmland were brought into the equation, views and vistas were considered along with the furniture and the *objets d'art*. Everything was designed for the changing lifestyle of the 18th century – The Golden Age.

The purpose of this book is to look at the Georgian house in its entirety, from the beauty of the house in its setting to the stylish ambiance of the interior. It is not meant to be an historical reference book, but an overview of a remarkable period, evoking a true sense of the style that is so loved and admired today and still emulated throughout the world.

*Henrietta Spencer-Churchill*

# ONE

# GEORGIAN STYLE

**T**HE GEORGIAN PERIOD is synonymous with the age of elegance. It spans the reigns of four King Georges, from the accession of George I in 1714 to the death of George IV in 1830. Stylistically speaking it lies between the heavy baroque of the 17th century and the bourgeois eclecticism of the 19th. Classic Georgian style was never static; it evolved throughout the century, veering between elegant restraint and exuberant ornamentation but always retaining its key elements – a commitment to quality and attention to detail.

# THE AGE OF ELEGANCE

THE GEORGIAN ERA was a relatively tranquil one that saw the rise of an affluent middle class and a sharp rise in house building. There was plenty of work for a large number of talented craftsmen who prided themselves on their skills. As a result, carpenters, cabinet-makers, stonemasons and metalworkers became wealthy and respected members of society. Many architects and craftsmen published collections of engraved designs for everything from a gatehouse to a staircase to a chair leg, and these pattern books were very influential in starting popular trends and ensuring a uniformity of the emerging styles.

In Georgian England, it was fashionable to be educated and to appreciate the arts. The practice of sending wealthy young aristocrats on a Grand Tour of Europe to complete their education led to a greater awareness of the legacy of ancient Greece and Rome, which was to be the principal catalyst for Georgian style. At the same time, growing numbers of people were made aware of these latest developments in architectural style, thanks to a proliferation of books and engravings on the subject.

The new squires and prosperous landowners were keen to keep up with the latest fashions and to increase the size and

*BELOW LEFT  This original gas lamp sconce is a typical example of late 18th-century wrought ironwork, traditionally painted in black and highlighted with gilt.*

*BELOW CENTRE  A good example of a late 18th-century verandah situated on the piano nobile of a Georgian terraced town house. The canopy is of lead and the frame of decorative ironwork.*

*BELOW RIGHT  An original, iron Georgian boot scraper decorated with the anthemion motif.*

scope of their estates to demonstrate their wealth and social prestige. For the wealthy, country life was almost idyllic and entertaining was carried out on a grand scale. Guests would often stay for weeks at a time and were expected to take advantage of all pursuits offered to them, from hunting and shooting to evenings of cards and music, dining and drinking. New roads and waterways helped to make this lifestyle practical, facilitating travel, trade and the exchange of ideas.

Many 18th-century squires were involved in politics and business that brought them into town for the all-important social season, leading to a building boom in the city, and resulting in the magnificent sweeps of uniform classical facades in terraces, crescents and squares that form the core of so much of the architecture we find familiar today.

This was a classical age, when everything from architecture to philosophy conformed to an idealism encompassing a lifestyle and taste that was characteristic of England at that time. It was a Golden Age, a time for prosperity to be openly expressed and enjoyed. The government of the day – the Whigs and their supporters – fostered the highest of moral and aesthetic values, and it is largely thanks to their idealism that the Georgian era produced such craftsmanship of the highest standards.

*BELOW RIGHT   An elaborate plasterwork medallion with swags and bows. Part of a series of wall plaques, this is typical of mid- to late-18th-century decorative plasterwork in the Adam style.*

*BELOW CENTRE   This oval staircase is lit from above by a domed skylight, a typical late 18th-century architectural feature.*

*BELOW LEFT   A George III bow-fronted sideboard with elegantly tapered legs, in mahogany with inlaid satinwood.*

# EARLY GEORGIAN 1714 — 1745

THE STYLE of the early Georgian period was inspired by the architecture of the early Roman Empire. The writings of the Roman architect Marcus Vitruvius Pollio describing the constructions and ornament of this period had intrigued scholars and artists from the Renaissance onwards, most famously the 16th-century Italian sculptor and architect Andrea Palladio, who provided the all-important engravings to explain the style. Palladio's *Four Books on Architecture* was first published in 1570, but had its resonance in 18th-century England through the efforts of the third Earl of Burlington who, following extensive travels in Italy, was keen to establish this style in Britain. He republished Palladio's works in 1715, determined to replace what he saw as the indiscipline and excesses of the baroque architects.

Palladianism became an instant success partly because it received the enthusiastic support of the newly-established Whig powerbase. The Whigs represented the new monied middle class and they adopted Palladianism (the ousted Tories had favoured the baroque style) as it so perfectly reflected their values of purity and idealism. The style adhered to the five classical orders: Tuscan, Doric, Ionic, Corinthian and Composite — the fundamental basis of classical architecture.

Emphasis was always on the symmetrical grand facade, often with a central pediment supported by columns or pilasters highlighting the importance of the first floor or *piano nobile*. Houses both large and small followed the same square or rectangular plan, with windows of equal size flanking the porticoed front door opening into a central hall with a vista that extended through to the garden beyond. Sash windows were favoured, and the Venetian or Palladian window (an arch flanked by two rectangular windows) situated above the front door, was a popular focal point.

Interiors followed the same strict classical principles in which proportions were expressed as ratios of a basic cube, and ornament was restricted to the classical orders and motifs such as the shell, acanthus leaf and Vitruvian scroll.

*RIGHT Portrait of* The Wollaston Family *in their impressive classically-proportioned drawing room, painted by William Hogarth in 1730.*

## MID-GEORGIAN 1745 – 1760

By THE MID-18TH CENTURY, fashionable Georgians were tiring of the constrictions of Palladianism and were actively looking for something a little more frivolous. Many embraced the French rococo style, which had its roots in 17th-century baroque – the French had never fallen for Palladianism. Although few interiors in England matched the extremes of the continent, rococo was nevertheless a big influence. It was a light, airy, asymmetrical style, favouring interiors ornamented with bright colours, complex scrollwork, naturalistic foliage, shell forms and asymmetric cartouches in giltwood and plasterwork.

The picturesque gothick style emerged as a particularly English version of rococo, springing from a love of romantic, ivy-clad ruins and should not be confused with the revival of the pure medieval Gothic style. Some of the earliest examples of the gothick were seen in garden temples and follies built around 1740. The style became popular for interiors, especially for rooms such as libraries where the gothick might be said to suggest a reverence for the past. Horace Walpole was an enthusiastic innovator, and Strawberry Hill, the house he had built in Twickenham in 1760, is a prime example of English gothick.

Alongside the gothick, there was a renewed enthusiasm for chinoiserie, inspired by exotic artefacts, fabrics and wallpapers imported from the Orient. Popular motifs included Chinese figures, dragons, pagodas, bells and latticework. This style was adopted by furniture designers, most notably Thomas Chippendale, and landscape designers – entire gardens were re-modelled in the style known as *Le Jardin Anglo-Chinois,* containing pagodas, oriental bridges and exotic plants. It was a delightfully frivolous style, much disapproved of by the more chauvinistic Georgian. However, chinoiserie was firmly entrenched, and remained popular until the end of the century, its swan song being the interior of the Brighton Pavilion created for the Prince Regent between 1802 and 1820.

*LEFT A painting by Francis Sartorius (1734–1804) of the second Earl of Aldborough and his wife in the grounds of Stratford Lodge, Baltinglass.*

# LATE GEORGIAN 1760 – 1800

THIS IS THE PERIOD OF NEOCLASSICISM, an inevitable revolt against the excesses of rococo. The principal figures were the Adam brothers, whose style was highly decorative, and James Wyatt and Henry Holland who worked in a more severe Greek style. Robert Adam and his brother James spent several years in Rome in the 1750s. Their work is an eclectic amalgamation of the antique world, taking inspiration from surviving buildings and artefacts of ancient Rome, Greece and the newly-excavated Pompeii and Herculaneum. The brothers used a new and vibrant palette of strong, bright colours and adopted Roman motifs of swags, festoons, griffins, chimeras, vases and urns. They published two volumes in the late 1770s, which inspired builders and their wealthy patrons to emulate their unique style.

Robert Adam specialized in transforming interiors with colours: strong pea-mint greens, bright pinks and blues and red/brown terracottas. He moved away from typical Georgian proportions, creating curved walls and domes and adding elaborate plasterwork. Adam left nothing to chance. Designing entire rooms from the cornices to the carpets, he worked closely with some of the great cabinet-makers and silversmiths of the period. James Wyatt, who borrowed his ideas freely from the Adam brothers, was a successful and fashionable architect whose Heveningham Hall in Suffolk is a superb example of classical Georgian style. Henry Holland was influenced by French classicism and the Louis XVI style; one of his most prestigious projects was Carlton House, a town house for the Prince Regent (later George IV).

Architects and builders at every point of the social and professional scale had a wide choice of styles and building materials available to them, and plenty of clients. Smaller houses, or 'villas', were built throughout the country to accommodate the rising middle class, while the nobility continued to build and to re-model their ancestral homes to make them less formal and severe.

RIGHT The Dutton Family, *painted by Johann Zoffany, relaxing at the card table in their drawing room. Bright colours, such as this turquoise, became popular during the later Georgian period.*

## REGENCY 1790 – 1830

THE REGENCY PERIOD saw the establishment of a style emphasising ease and comfort, perhaps reflecting the lifestyle of the Prince Regent himself. Interiors were plainer than in the late Georgian period, with less ornamental plasterwork and simpler architectural details. Colour became more important, and surfaces were decoratively painted with motifs from all over the world. Influences were eclectic: the French 'Empire' style of the Napoleonic era, the English gothick and a new passion for everything Egyptian, involving sphinxes, pyramids and hieroglyphs, but the strongest influence was perhaps the Greek revival, with its associated motifs such as the distinctive key pattern.

Furniture, which until the 1770s had been ranged around the walls, was now typically grouped in the middle of rooms, and many more pieces in the pared-down Regency style were being produced to accommodate a new style of living. Now there were sofa tables to read or write at, card tables and smaller, less formal, dining furniture that reflected new trends in entertaining.

Sir John Soane and John Nash were the Regency period's most influential architects, and Thomas Hope, who published *Household Furniture and Interior Decoration* in 1805, became an arbiter of style and taste, keeping craftsmen up to date with current trends.

The smaller houses, or villas, built in town and country, are some of the most charming results of the Regency style. Moving away from strict symmetry and incorporating bowed fronts and bay windows, they often have stuccoed exteriors where the creamy finish contrasts with a delicate confection of cast-ironwork canopies, balconies, verandahs and porches. These groups of villas, set in gardens, often along a winding road, were to be the pattern of future suburban development.

*RIGHT* Family Group In An Interior, *painted c. 1800 by a painter of the British school. The ladies, in their simple Empire-line white muslin dresses, and the gentlemen, in their figure-hugging jackets and long trousers, could have walked straight out of the pages of a Jane Austen novel. The simple lines of the furniture and the painted walls of the music room are typical of the Regency period.*

# TWO

# THE EXTERIOR

**W**ITH THE BUILDING of his house, the Georgian gentleman created more than a suitable home for his family, he expressed his position in society as a man of taste and wealth. The level of grandeur, in both scale and ornament, was therefore carefully judged to present a certain image to the world.

The result of this golden age of house building was a countryside dotted with the most delightful houses of exquisite proportions, built to the highest of standards.

## THE HOUSE IN ITS SETTING

*ABOVE AND TOP RIGHT Part of the mystique and beauty of a Georgian country house is the view of it from a distance. This Devon house is beautifully situated in a shallow valley and the aged brickwork and slate roof are enhanced by the lush background of woodland.*

I N THE 17TH CENTURY, gardens were seen as extensions of the grand baroque interiors, formal and symmetrical, with clipped yew hedges and a geometry of walks adorned with classical statuary and fountains. By the 18th century, a new style was emerging, influenced by the idealized classical landscapes of artists such as Claude Lorrain and Nicolas Poussin, and the descriptions of gardens in the works of the Roman poets Virgil and Horace.

Landscaped parks became the order of the day, with follies, temples, lakes, trees and rolling parklands created almost entirely by artifice. The ideal grounds for landscaping were uneven and sloping, preferably with a natural stream which

*BELOW RIGHT A typical symmetrical Georgian facade with external chimney stacks, which were common in early 18th-century houses. During the second half of the century and into the Regency period, the effect of stucco was much admired, as it gave houses a lightness and brightness.*

*BELOW A mid- to late-Georgian country house built from local stone, which has aged beautifully. The windows, with their narrow glazing bars and their proportions relating to the different floors of the house, are a classic example of Georgian architecture.*

could be dammed to provide lakes and canals. The ha-ha, or sunken fence, was used to separate garden from farmland, providing an uninterrupted vista from the house. Lawns were planted right up to the terrace of the house, and walks bordered with freely-growing greenery followed sinuous lines. Trees were planted in clumps or plantations to further improve the view from the house, and the houses themselves were built in commanding positions or nestled into high ground in order to benefit from the aesthetics of the newly-created landscaped parkland.

The architect William Kent and the gardener Charles Bridgeman, working at the beginning of the century, were the pioneers of this 'artinatural' style, followed in the mid-18th century by Lancelot 'Capability' Brown, whose advice was sought by many of the great country landowners. His love of water and trees and his understanding of scale were most notably incorporated into the sweeping settings he created for Blenheim Palace. 'Capability' Brown's successor was Humphry Repton, who re-introduced the flower garden, an element that had been unfashionable for decades.

*BELOW This impressive country house was re-modelled in 1770 by Sir Robert Taylor, a London architect. Its charming polygonal bay would have made the most of the spectacular views over the picturesque grounds and the rolling Devon countryside.*

*LEFT  Built in 1803, this two-
storeyed Regency country house
has five bays across the frontage.
The hipped roof, partially concealed by the parapet, would have
accommodated the servants' floor.
The porch is supported on columns
of the Tuscan order and embellished
with a cast-iron balcony. The
rusticated quoins, or corner stones,
add to the imposing nature of this
facade. The house is strategically
situated, offering magnificent
views down a valley.*

*ABOVE* A typical Georgian crescent of terraced houses in Bath. The centre two houses with the pediment form the focal point of the grandiose sweep. It is possible that originally these two houses were built as one. The architectural details of the houses are typical of the mid- to late-Georgian facade.

## TOWN TERRACES

INSPIRED BY THE CLASSICAL architecture of Italy, Inigo Jones built the first uniform terraced housing in the Covent Garden Piazza in the 1630s. The terrace became the perfect solution for urban housing. For the most wealthy inhabitants, a terrace could provide a well-appointed house within a palatial facade, as in Queen Square in Bath, begun by John Wood in 1728, or Bedford Square in London, begun in 1775. Linking the grand squares, terraces of correspondingly smaller houses with less ornamentation were built for those of more modest means, and the Georgian townscape developed the order and symmetry we so admire today.

The appearances of terraces changed over the Georgian period as town planning developed in sophistication and some of the great architects of the time applied themselves to the task. Where local stone was available, as in Bath and Edinburgh, terraces were stone clad, but in cities such as London and Dublin, terraces were built in brick with elegant ornamentation to enhance the basic form. Central pediments and columns were added, giving long terraces a much grander overall appearance. Stucco was introduced in the 1770s, transforming the brick facades into a smooth, stone-like appearance. Coade stone, an artificial stone which could economically simulate the effect of elaborate carving, was applied to door surrounds, and decorative metalwork, which was now being produced in large quantities, was used for architectural details such as balconies, railings, lampholders and the delicate tracery on fanlights.

Towns expanded not according to a grid system, but taking account of the topography of the area. The new town of Edinburgh, for instance, was built looking out over the Old Town and the Firth of Forth, and the later circuses and crescents on the hills rising out of Bath were built so the residents could benefit from the spectacular views.

*ABOVE RIGHT In this Georgian crescent, again in Bath, the main rooms on the* piano nobile *are given emphasis by the columns, which continue up to the second floor, framing the windows. The facade is built using a warm, honey-coloured stone from a local quarry, which is very typical of houses in the Bath area.*

## VILLAGE HOUSES

*LEFT A typical Georgian stone village house like this was built for the burgeoning middle classes. There is little ornament apart from the broken pediment canopy over the door and the string course which divided the ground floor from the upper floors.*

IN THE THOUSANDS of villages of Britain there are often groups of modest Georgian houses in which the doctor, lawyer and rector would have lived. Scaled-down versions of their grander cousins, they present symmetrical, orderly exteriors with perhaps a small flourish in the form of a pedimented porch or carved dentil under the roof. Jane Austen in *Sense and Sensibility* describes such a house: 'Barton Cottage, though small, was comfortable and compact…On each side of the entrance was a sitting room about sixteen feet square…beyond them…the offices and stairs.'

On some of the grandest of Georgian estates, an entire new village would be built to house estate workers, as existing cottages had been demolished to rationalize farming methods and to create the perfect 18th-century landscape. Often built to a plan and design suggested by the architect working on the main house, they were usually placed with due formality outside the gates to the park.

The end of the century saw the rise of the 'picturesque village' – a collection of *cottages ornés* randomly grouped around a village green. Individuality was the theme of the day and it was quite common to find a whitewashed thatched cottage next door to a little lattice-windowed gothick folly. It gave the wealthy landowner a chance to show himself as a philanthropist of taste and fashion. The first picturesque village was Blaise Hamlet, built outside Bristol in 1810 to designs by the Prince Regent's favourite architect, John Nash.

*ABOVE LEFT A row of 18th-century cottages. This was a period of gradual improvement in living conditions for estate workers, although many landlords were more interested in a picturesque exterior appearance than the convenience of the interior.*

## LODGES AND GATEHOUSES

FIRST IMPRESSIONS ARE IMPORTANT, and the Georgian gatehouse was built to impress the visitor rather than to provide comfortable accommodation for the gatekeeper. As most of the grander houses could not be seen from the road, the lodge or gatehouse was also a way of informing visitors of the main entrance to the estate. They were usually built as part of a grand scheme that included the main house and the surrounding parklands. On the outside, they may have carried a coat of arms or fine architectural details reminiscent of the style of the main house, or the owner may have decided to proclaim himself as a man of fashion by building his gatehouse in one of the more fanciful architectural styles such as rococo, gothick or Regency picturesque. The insides, however, were uniformly plain and modest, often only on one level with small rooms.

Smaller lodges, which were not always inhabited, were built at secondary entrances to the estate. Many of them incorporated a set of wrought-iron gates or at least a cattle grid to keep the estate livestock from wandering.

*FAR LEFT The lodge attached to the main entrance at Downhill in Northern Ireland, originally inhabited by a gatekeeper. No expense has been spared in the gothick ornamentation of the stonework with its rustication, corner columns and pinnacles.*

*BELOW This glorious early Georgian gate in the form of a triumphal arch is impressively ornamented with rustication, balustrading and a gable surmounted with urn finials. For all its grandeur it made an inconvenient dwelling — the gatekeeper had to live either side of the arch.*

## WALLED GARDENS

IN MEDIEVAL TIMES the kitchen garden was located near to the house and planted in a systematic manner with a practical selection of vegetables and herbs. By the 18th century, as landscape gardening developed and knowledge of plants increased, areas close to the house were reserved for sweet-smelling flowers and impressive imported species. The scent of herbs and vegetables and the sight of squads of gardeners were considered to be undesirable, so kitchen gardens were moved and placed near the stables where they could interfere neither with the ideal planned landscape nor with the delicate sensibilities of the owners and their guests.

High brick or stone walls provided shelter from the weather and protection from marauding wildlife and were sometimes ornamented with strategically-placed openings through which controlled vistas could be admired. Southern

*BELOW These arches form part of the elaborate garden plan designed by William Kent at Rousham in Oxfordshire. The garden slopes down to the river, combining natural vistas with architectural focal points.*

*BELOW A beautiful herbaceous border backs onto a walled kitchen garden. The stone wall provides a backdrop for climbing plants and flowers. Time has given the stone and brickwork the character that only natural ageing can bring.*

*RIGHT  Even in a forgotten and neglected condition, stonework retains a lovely texture. The gate was clearly devised to keep small animals out of a kitchen garden.*

walls were especially important for growing peaches, as the bricks, warmed by the sun during the day, retained heat and continued ripening the fruit after sundown.

The typical kitchen garden was laid out with systematic rows of planting, and a herb garden where plants were intricately entwined to produce a glorious combination of colour, pattern and scent. Box hedges delineated the separate areas, which were usually designed in a four-square plan with straight paths (easier to work in) and an ornamental feature such as a pond or sundial in the centre to provide a focal point. With all this attention to aesthetics, the very gardens that had been hidden away from general view soon became popular destinations for tranquil retreat.

*BELOW  A terrace and water feature in the spirit of the Regency garden. By the turn of the 19th century, the area surrounding the house was regarded as an extension of the interior. Conservatories were an innovation of this period.*

*RIGHT  The walled garden had been a feature of country houses for centuries, but became newly fashionable at the end of the 18th century. Ladies and gentlemen were increasingly interested in horticulture and enjoyed visiting the kitchen gardens.*

## WATER FEATURES

FROM 1715 ONWARDS, formal gardens in the French style became less popular and a passion for natural landscapes evolved. The great landscape architects of the time considered water an essential element of the Georgian parkland. Lancelot 'Capability' Brown created the magnificent lake at Blenheim from a modest stream; Vanbrugh transformed many a view by damming streams to create cascades and flooding marshes to form lakes, and William Kent created gentle serpentine streams and embellished the natural shape of rivers to form areas leading to and from the riverbank.

One of the most inspired of 18th-century gardens is at Stourhead in Wiltshire, where streams were dammed and fishponds joined together to form a free-form lake. The owner, Henry Hoare, created the garden over a period of thirty years without the help of professional designers.

*ABOVE  This attractive brick-built village house is perfectly situated across from a village green and a pond. The symmetrical facade is reflected in the water, emphasising the perfect proportions of the house.*

*FAR LEFT  A house situated in a commanding position in the Devon countryside. The columns of the front porch form a perfect frame from which the eye is led onto the terrace, to the steps flanked by urns, and on to the river below.*

LEFT AND BELOW  This attractively solid stone staircase and balustrade leads down towards the river and to a grotto in the grounds, which were designed by William Kent. The stone has aged naturally to give a rich variation and depth of colour.

RIGHT  Box hedges are used in this walled garden to provide a series of interesting shapes of flower beds for roses and other typically English flowers. Walkways provide a good contrast of texture against the greenery. The stable block in the background was designed by William Kent.

# INFORMAL GARDENS

MANY A GRAND ESTATE has an area where nature is allowed to take its course, but the informal flower garden is generally associated with the English country cottage and village house. The typical small Georgian garden would bloom with roses, honeysuckle, lavender, hollyhocks, primroses, hawthorn, lilac and laburnum. Adventurous gardeners swapped ideas and cuttings as imported specimens such as rhododendrons, azaleas, magnolias, camellias, carnations, auriculas, tulips and anemones were introduced from China, the Americas and Australia.

Such gardens were a riot of colourful planting, with little consideration given to layout. The passion for the planned small garden did not develop until well into the 19th century.

*LEFT, RIGHT AND BELOW The great landscape gardener, Humphry Repton (d. 1818), ended his days living contentedly in a cottage which he described as 'a dwelling where happiness may reside unsupported by wealth'. He realized that gardens were not only for show but also for enjoyment and for the production of vegetables and fruit. To screen the less elegant aspects of the garden, he recommended that fruit trees should be trained with arches and infilled with trellis. He also advocated gravel paths so that the garden could be perambulated in comfort. This was a time when gardening became much more interesting as the number of available species vastly increased thanks to Georgian travellers and plantsmen exploring hitherto unknown territories in North America and China.*

## GARDEN BUILDINGS

THE INCIDENTAL GARDEN BUILDING was an essential feature of the landscape garden, providing both a focal point in the grand scheme of things and a shady spot to take refreshment on a summer's afternoon or to sit in quiet, reflective peace to write a poem. The design of these buildings either followed that of the house or, if added later by a landscape gardener, one of the fashionable revivals such as chinoiserie, or gothick – the popular romantic medieval look which led to a proliferation of ruined castles and crumbling follies. Gardener's cottages and dovecotes were also disguised as classical temples or rustic hermitages.

The stable block – an essential addition to every house – was usually designed for function rather than style. They were often built around a courtyard with a cobbled ground and included a clock tower and accommodation for the grooms.

*BELOW The Georgian taste for the exotic could be given full rein in the creation of garden buildings, which were designed purely for amusement in any frivolous architectural style of the moment. This little garden temple at Sezincote, Gloucestershire, has an appropriately oriental flavour since the first owner of the house was an Indian Nabob.*

*RIGHT This polygonal tower at Studley Royal in Yorkshire is a whimsical mongrel of both classical and gothick styles. The tower is positioned to overlook the magnificent landscaped gardens, which were among the most famous of the age, and had the genuine and spectacular Gothic ruin of Fountains Abbey as an eye-catching backdrop.*

*RIGHT  A sundial, no doubt strategically placed by the resident gardener, is situated above a doorway leading into a walled garden.*

*BELOW LEFT AND RIGHT  Two views showing the focal point of an old-fashioned walled garden. The simple timber-framed pergola acts as a climing frame for several species of rose and provides a colourful centrepiece from all four walkways. The gravel paths are bordered by boxwood hedges.*

BELOW *This beautiful stone wall with a strategically placed round opening frames a vista from the walled kitchen garden towards the less formal areas beyond. The old stone wall is a perfect backdrop for growing soft fruits, such as plums and damsons, that require shelter and sun.*

LEFT *A romantic stone statue provides the perfect focal point at the end of a tree-lined walkway. The gravel path is bordered by rolling lawns.*

*RIGHT* A wooden garden bench with a latticework back. This patterning was considered to be rather Chinese in style.

*BELOW* A cast-iron bench in the gothick style. Georgian garden furniture was often painted green.

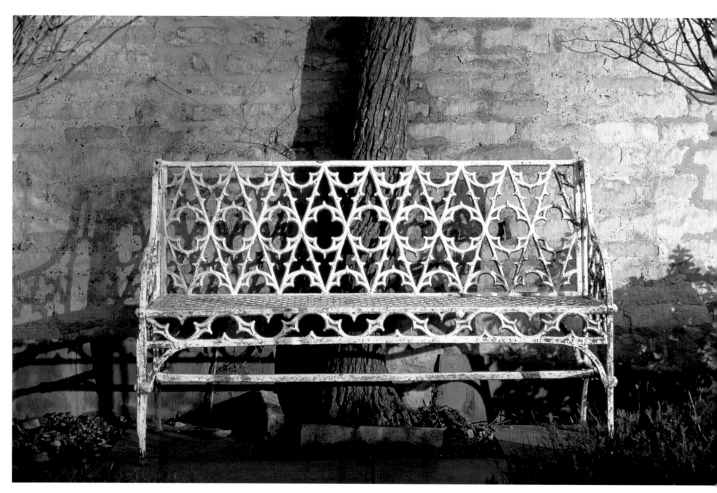

## GARDEN FURNITURE

THE 18TH-CENTURY country house garden was designed for leisure and pleasure, and in order to rest and admire its splendours, garden seats and benches were installed at strategic points. Until the introduction in the 1760s of Coade stone, which is non-porous and therefore resistant to frost damage, most stone benches were made from locally-quarried stone. Early stone benches were simple in style; the straight slab seat, perhaps with a moulded edge, supported on carved plinths reflecting a design used on the outside of the main house, such as acanthus leaves or a family crest.

Wooden seats and benches, often with latticed or fretwork backs, were very typical. Ironwork seats were popular too. Sometimes they were custom-built by the local blacksmith to fit around a tree base – other designs incorporated wheels so they could be moved from place to place for the convenience of ladies watching garden games. Some benches thoughtfully incorporated hinged footrests to prevent the ladies getting their skirts muddy.

*BELOW A shallow, semi-circular stone bench with magnificent decorative urns at either end. Backdrops of dark hedges complement the mellow tones of stonework and were frequently used to frame statuary, sundials and other stone features.*

## IRONWORK AND ENTRANCES

WROUGHT IRON was first used in Britain around 450 B.C. but it is a slow and time-consuming art, so when the cheaper and quicker cast-iron process was introduced in the mid-18th century, structural and decorative ironwork quickly gained in popularity.

At the start of the Georgian era, ironwork was very much a city material used for railings, gates, lampirons, balconies and boot scrapers. Early railings had simple, heavy uprights with finials in the shape of arrows, thistles or pineapples. Ironwork was usually painted black and, in grander settings, picked out with gold leaf. During the Regency period, ironwork motifs included Adam's favourite anthemions, palmettes, swags and urns. Cast-iron verandahs, porches and canopies became popular architectural features in both town and country.

*BELOW LEFT AND RIGHT These two gates, both of which lead to walled gardens, are fine examples of Georgian decorative ironwork. The ornamentation reflects the motifs used on the surrounding stonework, making the gates arresting focal points, while allowing a view through to the colourful planting beyond.*

*RIGHT These fine, sturdy stone gateposts topped with carved stone balls make an impressive entrance to a Georgian country manor house. The original wrought-iron gates have been removed for practical reasons, but even without them, the gateposts stand as an architectural feature, framing the park beyond.*

## ROOFS

BEFORE 1707, most roofs were steeply pitched with prominent wooden eaves and cornices. Regulations introduced after the Great Fire of London banned the use of wood as a safety precaution, resulting in roofs becoming lower in pitch, often hipped, and partly hidden behind a parapet wall with cornices made from stone or brick.

By the late 18th century, a pronounced hipped roof was introduced to provide extra living accommodation in the attic space. This was known as the mansard roof and it incorporated two different pitches, with dormer windows in the lower pitch. In grand houses, cornices were elaborately decorated and the parapet often featured balustrades in the Palladian manner.

The position of chimney stacks is often a good indication of the date of a house. In the 16th and 17th centuries, chimneys were usually sited in the centre. As part of the Georgian trend for re-modelling and updating, they were replaced by end stacks, and later still the projection of the stacks was contained within the building, so only the pots were visible.

Clay tiles were the principal roofing material throughout the 18th century. Made at local brickworks, their colour was determined by the colour of the local clay, giving rise to regional differences. Pantiles, roofing tiles that interlock so they could be laid on roofs without pegs or nails, were originally imported from Holland and were first used in the eastern counties of England at the beginning of the 18th century. They were most popular for low-pitched roofs and simple roofs with a light framework.

Stone slates were thick and heavy, requiring a strong roof structure, but they had the advantage of ageing beautifully, providing a distinctive look for stone-built houses and fitting in perfectly with local surroundings. They were common in the north of England and along the limestone belt that stretches from the Cotswolds down to Sussex. Welsh blue-grey slates became prevalent, particularly in towns and cities, in the second half of the 18th century. They were produced in a variety of sizes and shapes and, being much lighter than stone, were easily transported around the country via the improved network of canals and waterways.

*ABOVE AND FAR RIGHT Attention to detail was the hallmark of the Georgian builder. Here, the dormer windows of the attic floor add interest and height to the simple pitched roof. The fine detailing of the cornice can be seen in the detail above.*

## DOORS

THE CHARACTERISTIC Georgian exterior door is beautifully proportioned, panelled and always painted. It is set in an architectural door case that incorporates a fanlight or transom to admit light into the hallway beyond.

The doorcase was often the main, or only, area for ornament and elaboration on a facade, so it tended to be as fashionable as possible. Early Georgian doors had projecting square canopies supported on classical brackets with pilasters

LEFT  *The front door of a country property. The six-panelled door has glazed upper panels and a fanlight above. The painted columns are a typical feature of the Georgian entrance porch.*

BELOW  *The porch and front door of a late Georgian house. The glazing bars are fine and the glazed upper sections allow light to penetrate the hall. The stone is a local sandstone — note how the patina on the columns has lightened with age.*

or columns. Triangular or segmental pediments, perhaps enriched with classical friezes, became popular by the 1730s. During the Adam period, the fashionable door opening was arched and accentuated with an elaborate keystone. Fanlights were introduced from about 1720 and by the mid-18th century, they had become very decorative, the metalwork patterning reflecting styles of the period – rococo swirls and fan patterns were very popular.

The door itself normally had six panels connected by rails (crosspieces) and styles (vertical pieces). As with all architectural features in Georgian houses, proportion played an important part in the layout of the panels. The top two were the smallest, the middle two slightly larger and the bottom pair, set below the doorknob, were larger still.

Early doorknobs were plain iron, but the passion for detail in the later period saw the introduction of elaborate doorknockers in the form of masks, griffins and urns.

*BELOW A town house front door with a decorative fanlight that allows natural daylight to filter through into the house. The simple panelled doors are painted. Double doors make a particularly attractive first impression.*

*BELOW The attractively arched front door of a country house. The shape of the fanlight follows that of the stonework, and the door is divided into three parts, the top section split into twelve glazed panes.*

## WINDOWS

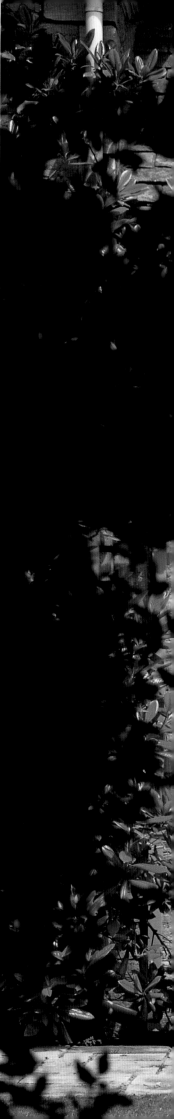

T HE QUINTESSENTIAL Georgian sash window is one of the finest characteristics of British houses from this period. Unlike earlier casement and mullion windows, the double-hung sash added a new elegance to the facade of town and country houses and soon became a status symbol.

The particular style of Georgian windows was due in part to new Building Acts (memories of the Great Fire gave rise to these regulations) which stipulated that wooden frames must be recessed from the facade, and in part to Georgian glass technology. Early windows have small, heavy panes and

*RIGHT  Delicately interlaced glazing bars on an arched window – typical of late 18th- and early 19th-century windows.*

*FAR RIGHT  The facade of a mid-Georgian property, a good example of well-proportioned ground- and first-floor windows. Simple carved stone architraves frame the windows, and the upper ones are emphasised with carved pediments. The beautiful roof is made of Cotswold stone slates.*

therefore thick glazing bars. Window openings were small and it was common for the upper half to be fixed and only the lower half to open. At first these sections were kept open by pegs until the introduction of cords, weights and pulleys, which were cleverly disguised in sash boxes behind the frame. Glass and windows were both subject to tax during this period, which is why some houses have bricked-up windows and others have dummy windows painted on the front to preserve the external symmetry while saving money.

The overall style of the window and its panes changed according to the fashions of the time, and the size of individual windows reflected the importance of the rooms behind, so in houses where the principal rooms were on the *piano nobile,* the first-floor windows were taller and grander than the rest.

Sash windows are described by the number of panes in the upper and lower sashes – thus a four over four has four panes in each sash and a four over six has four in the upper and six

in the lower. The most common size in the mid-Georgian period was six over six. As the period progressed, glass-making became more sophisticated and larger, thinner panes were being produced, which in turn led to larger window openings and slender, more elaborate glazing bars, culminating in the Regency bay and the door-length french window. Light, a precious commodity in those days, could now flood into the house.

In the Regency period, glazing patterns became more elaborate, panes were given Gothic shapes and margin lights – the narrow panes set at the borders of windows – were often filled with blue and amber coloured glass.

In the early Georgian period, windows might be accentuated on the exterior by an architectural frame with a triangular pediment or by quoins or different-coloured brickwork. In the later period it was more likely to be a delicate ironwork balcony, especially for full-length first-floor windows, providing both ornament and safety.

*LEFT An example of a Regency coloured-glass window from a garden building.*

*BELOW A typical symmetrical sash, set back into a recess and framed with a stone architrave.*

*BELOW A Venetian or Palladian window with fixed side windows and a centre working sash. These windows were a favourite feature throughout the Georgian period, and would often be centred over the front door.*

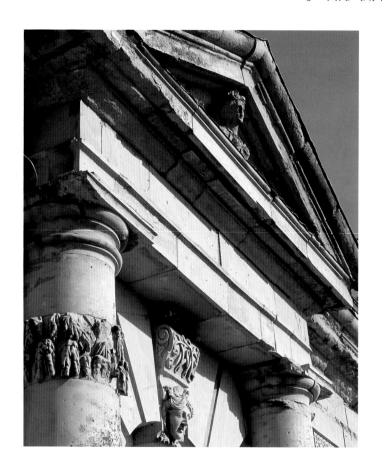

*LEFT  The wonderfully crisp details on this exterior demonstrate the remarkable skill of the Georgian stonemason. Unfortunately, some stones, Bath stone in particular, are very susceptible to the damaging effects of weathering and pollution.*

*RIGHT  A wrought-ironwork flourish decorates this torch snuffer at the door of a Bath terrace house. In the dark of a Georgian night, linkboys used flaming torches to lead citizens through the streets to the safety of their homes.*

*RIGHT  A typically Regency canopied balcony of cast iron. These are sometimes referred to as Trafalgar balconies since they were popular at the time the battle was won.*

*BELOW* Two examples of the decorative use of the mask motif, effective both as a drainpipe support and as a keystone.

*RIGHT AND BELOW RIGHT* Houses were given a show of grandeur by using heavily rusticated stonework on the ground level.

# THREE

# THE INTERIOR

THE GEORGIAN INTERIOR is typified by a formal symmetry enlivened with decorative motifs that came in and out of fashion as the 18th century progressed. The century started with a classical revival in which interiors, virtually devoid of unnecessary ornament, faithfully reflected the strict symmetry of the exterior. By the mid-Georgian period interior design had firmly distanced itself from strict architectural principles and enjoyed dalliances with a variety of decorative motifs ranging from rococo curlicues, gothick arches and Chinese lattices to festoons of fruit and Roman urns.

*LEFT* Georgian hallways were designed to impress the visitor with the owner's obvious wealth and good taste. Simple Doric columns frame a doorway into this imposing classical rotunda with an original ironwork hall lantern, enclosed with glass to protect the candles from draughts.

*BELOW* Detail of the steps showing the technical brilliance of the Georgian builder. These slim stone slabs, with their simply carved tread ends, have been cantilevered off the wall to free up the space beneath.

*LEFT* The niches in the walls of the stair well were originally designed to display classical statues and busts. The graceful lines of the cantilevered staircase, accentuated by the sweep of the mahogany banister rail, are happily unencumbered by pillars and supporting beams.

*BELOW* Daylight floods in through a skylight set into a coffered dome. Coffering, a technique using ornamented recessed panels to form a pattern, was a Roman idea most famously found at the Pantheon, and beloved of Andrea Palladio.

*LEFT* The entrance hall as a sitting room. This grandly colonnaded Palladian hall with its magnificently decorative ceiling is hardly cosy, but certainly impressive. A double staircase rises to upper floors from the staircase hall beyond, visible through the arched openings.

*ABOVE* The principal rooms lead off this hall, which has been well-equipped for visitors. There are comfortable chairs, a welcoming fireplace and books to read, but the principal function of the room is as a glorified passageway, so furniture is sensibly placed to allow for ease of circulation.

## ENTRANCE HALLS

DURING THE 18TH CENTURY, the hall grew in importance thanks to the advent of Palladianism, when the entrance hall was for the first time combined with the staircase to create one large imposing space. Staircases had previously been tucked into walls or, in grander houses, situated in separate staircase halls. The Georgian entrance hall was designed to set the tone of the house and to create an impressive and awe-inspiring vestibule where visitors would wait to ascend to the *piano nobile* and be received into the saloon, dining room or parlours above.

*ABOVE AND FAR RIGHT  The hallway of a small town house in Bath. The panelling detail of the narrow, but beautifully proportioned front door matches the under-stair panelling. The practical fold-down table is original, and the formal, un-upholstered x-frame stools are typical of the hall furniture of the period. The walls are hung with a collection of mezzo-tints — a popular medium for social satire in the late 18th century.*

Town houses had to make do with whatever space was available, and the width of the hall was always an indicator of the grandeur of the house. In terraced town houses, the staircase sometimes spiralled up the back, but more usually it ascended directly from the front door.

In houses grand and modest, the style and treatment of the entrance hall closely followed the style of the house. Palladian halls were notable for their lack of colour and the emphasis placed on architectural features. They were not warm and inviting places, although many would have had a fireplace — a good example is Houghton Hall in Norfolk, the home of Sir Robert Walpole. Hall furniture was heavy and imposing, rarely upholstered, and made much use of heraldic crests and coats of arms.

Robert Adam was triumphant in creating the neoclassical style in halls such as those at Syon House and Kedleston, where the use of huge marble columns coupled with delicate plasterwork and decoration achieves a wonderful balance of grandeur and style. A feature of the Palladian hall in town and country was the skylight or dome, which threw light down the entire stairwell, highlighting the shape of the staircase.

*RIGHT AND BELOW RIGHT* An early 18th-century staircase with thick, turned wooden balusters of alternating styles. The treads are finished with elaborate carving, which ties in with the panelling in the hall and up the staircase. The half-glazed front door has working shutters, providing additional security. The brass box lock is a restored original.

*FAR RIGHT* The hall floor of a Georgian country house was typically of stone or marble, with no rugs on the floor and no carpeting on the stairs. This spacious hall has a stone floor with insets of slate. The elegant panelling running up the stairwell is all the decoration required, obviating the need for paintings or prints.

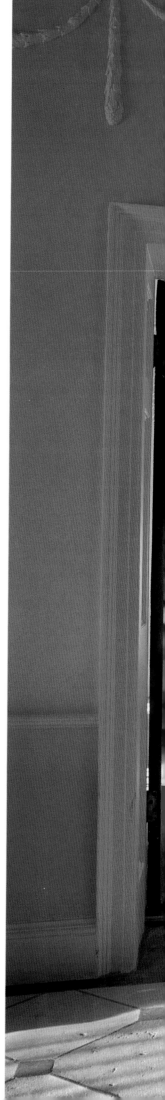

Once the principal rooms were no longer situated on the first floor, the staircase lost its architectural prominence and the hall became a vestibule by the main entrance, made comfortable by a fireplace and seating. In smaller houses and villas the hall was obviously more modest in scale, reflecting the lifestyle of the occupants. The aim was not to impress but to provide easy access and a warm welcome.

*ABOVE AND FAR LEFT  The staircase and architectural details are all new, but typical of the late 18th century. The floor is of York stone with slate insets and the stone staircase replaces an earlier wooden one.*

## DRAWING ROOMS

THE TERM 'DRAWING ROOM' developed in the 16th century, and referred to a room to which the owner of the house could withdraw to find privacy and quiet. It was a room sometimes used for taking the occasional meal and for sitting and relaxing after a meal with a game of cards or a good book. In houses without state rooms or saloons for entertaining, the drawing room was the principal room for receiving guests.

Since the Regency period a drawing room has meant a general living room, and a place where ladies could retire after dinner while the men stayed in the dining room drinking port and recounting stories. In smaller houses, it was common for the drawing room to be situated on the ground floor close to the entrance and near the dining room. In larger Palladian houses and terraced town houses, the principal rooms were on the first floor or *piano nobile,* and

*FAR LEFT The proportions of Georgian homes give the principal rooms an enviable elegance. There is no need to correct them, just to play to their strengths. In this room, subtle shades of green emphasize the beautiful proportions of the panelling.*

*BELOW Original gems of Georgian furniture among the comfortable modern seating include the pretty piecrust tea table, the work boxes either side of the fireplace and the Adam-style giltwood mirror over the marble mantle.*

*LEFT, BELOW LEFT AND RIGHT* This elegant 18th-century drawing room has had many of the original architectural features and plasterwork replaced, and a dado rail has been added to enhance the proportions. Woodwork and plasterwork are painted in three tones of off-white and the walls above and below the dado are stippled and dragged. The elegant window treatments bring luxury and colour into the room, at the same time respecting the beautiful arched shape of the windows. The colour scheme is based around the muted shades of the Savonnerie rug, and all the objects and furniture are carefully selected, genuine period pieces.

the dining room and drawing room would be next to each other, connected by double doors. Large windows looking over a verandah were a common feature and, as glass-making technology improved towards the end of the century, the windows became taller, often extending to the floor.

The drawing room was very much the ladies' domain and consequently reflected a feminine style in terms of decoration. Early in the 18th century, walls were wood panelled and painted or had an oak-panelled wainscot (the area between the skirting board and the dado rail) and either paint or wallpaper above. It was fashionable to paint the panelling in striking colours or to commission decorative plasterwork for the walls, which would have been painted off-white, and in grander homes, detailed in gilt.

At that time, few people owned significant numbers of paintings and so decorative wall treatments were important.

*LEFT A typical mid-18th-century marble-topped side table with chinoiserie fretwork detailing. Side tables were designed to fit against walls and often the backs were left completely plain. The urn is another typically Georgian decorative item.*

*LEFT This decorative double tassel tie-back was made to order, along with the curtain fringe, to enhance the rich, silk damask curtain fabric. The tassel is made from silk to a design that was frequently used in the later part of the 18th century.*

LEFT  *This light, double aspect sitting room is part of a later addition to a Georgian property. The architectural details, such as the plaster cornice, ceiling mouldings and carved fireplace have been carefully matched to the mid-Georgian style of the rest of the house. The walls are stippled in a soft apricot colour taken from the curtain fabric. The walnut bureau bookcase and the side tables are geniune Georgian, helping to add an authentic feel to this contemporary room.*

*FAR RIGHT Panelling typical of the early Georgian period when paintings were not so prevalent and the wall decoration had to speak for itself. The long case clock, with its elaborate hood topped with brass finials, is also typical of the early 18th century.*

*BELOW Early Georgian wooden mantels did not always incorporate a shelf. They were often conceived as part of the panelling detail.*

Later still, panelling above the dado rail was omitted altogether and the walls were upholstered with damask, cut velvet, silk or flock wallpaper, which left a better expanse of wall space on which to hang paintings acquired on the Grand Tour or commissioned from the thriving British school. Ceilings tended to be plastered, with a more or less elaborate cornice, the size and detail of the plasterwork depending on the grandeur and scale of the room.

At the beginning of the Georgian period, furniture was sparse and placed around the edges of the room. In grander houses, certain pieces of furniture would have been designed specifically for the room by the architect or by one of the prominent designers such as Chippendale, Hepplewhite or Sheraton. In more modest homes the furniture would also be

ABOVE, RIGHT AND BELOW *The drawing room of a Georgian country house built c. 1800. The most striking features are the beautiful full-length windows so typical of the period. Through the windows can just be seen the delicate tracery of the cast-iron verandah which fronts the house. Once window openings became larger, curtains naturally became an important element in interior decoration, and these exceptional examples were made of silk using an authentic pattern from the Regency period. Fine examples of period furniture include the gilt shell-headed mirror, the Sheraton side chair (above) and the beautiful mid-Georgian secretaire on the right of the main picture. The delicate hand-painted cornice is decorated with festoons echoed in the drapery of the curtains, and the walls below the dado rail are elegantly marbled.*

*LEFT  A corner of the drawing room shown on the previous pages. Screens were used to protect seating areas from draughts, and this delightful example is decorated with 18th-century topographical prints. Logs are stored in a Regency wine cooler, and a tea tray is set with Georgian silver and porcelain.*

specially selected for the room and made by local craftsmen using one of the many pattern books available. Early Georgian furniture was more delicate than the heavy oak style of the baroque period, and was made from lighter woods such as walnut, maple and yew. In 1721 import duty was lifted from mahogany and this lovely wood soon became the wood most associated with the Georgian period, especially after France stopped exporting walnut following a severe winter which destroyed many of the trees. Georgian furniture was practical as well as beautiful. There were tripod tables with hinged tops

*ABOVE  The Print Room was a mid-Georgian decorative craze, and this is typical of a Print Room wall. Engravings or prints were stuck directly onto walls, their trompe l'oeil frames together with ropes and tassels painted around them. The box on the side table is a lined gentleman's dressing box.*

that could be placed flat against the wall when not in use, and chairs and sofas that were as comfortable as they were stylish. Side tables, card tables and writing desks were designed to fulfil the varied needs of this leisured society. One of the most fashionable of pastimes was the drinking of tea. Prepared in the drawing room by the lady of the house, it was a ritual that occurred several times a day. The fashion accordingly led to the production of many tea-related items, from inlaid tea tables to kettle stands.

*LEFT An idiosyncratic drawing room in an Irish country house. The scrolling rococo foliage at cornice level has been picked out in gilt and the walls are decorated with cut-outs in the Print Room style, a fashion that took off in the 1760s.*

*ABOVE As a rule, fabric was only used on the walls of very grand rooms and, from the middle of the century onwards, was superseded in the popular taste by wallpapers. The lovely yellow of this brocade gives extra sparkle to the gilded frames and furniture.*

LEFT *Mahogany was the favoured wood of the mid-18th century, and this is a lovely collection of furniture of that period, from the round table and the Hepplewhite-style chairs to the glazed bureau bookcase, which makes an ideal display cabinet for the collection of antique porcelain.*

The fireplace was of major importance as a source both of heat and light – a precious commodity before the advent of efficient oil lamps. Furniture was designed specifically for use around a fireplace, in particular the fire screen, usually with a mahogany frame and an inset – a painted or embroidered panel. Mirrors were hung over mantles to help reflect light from the fire and from surrounding candle sconces, and were often incorporated with surrounds of plasterwork or panelling, into the design of the fireplace itself.

Floors were generally of polished wood, either made from oak or, later on, mahogany. Rugs and carpets were expensive and not much seen during the early part of the century, although if there was a good rug  to be found in the house, it would most certainly have been in the drawing room. As more Oriental rugs were imported and as factories such as Axminster and Wilton started production, architects became

BELOW *A lovely mid-18th-century sitting room with an early Georgian wing chair, original candle sconces and a lovely carved marble fire surround. The fender and firescreen are later additions. Antique furniture and leather-bound books give the room a wonderful ambiance.*

*BELOW Adam-inspired plasterwork festoons adorn the walls of this elegant, small sitting room. The Adam-style fireplace has a low fender and coal basket modelled on Georgian originals.*

involved in designing rugs for rooms. Robert Adam, for instance, was particularly noted for his carpets.

Festoon curtains, which were common in French rococo houses, became popular once the fashion for curves and swirls arrived in England. Straighter lines were introduced during the neoclassical period and lasted until the Regency, when tastes changed again in favour of lavish window treatments often incorporating several sets of curtains, richly adorned with fringes and tassels.

*RIGHT The generous gilt over-mantel mirror enhances the lovely proportions of this elegant sitting room. Window treatments are given emphasis by the carved giltwood curtain cornice.*

## DINING ROOMS

*LEFT The dining room of a Georgian country house viewed from the hall. The walls are painted a rich Pompeiian red, matching early paint scrapings found under subsequent layers of paint and wallpaper. Dining rooms were the place to hang family portraits, and the tradition has been continued here. The dumb waiter in the centre holds silver salt cellars and pepper pots for the table.*

DURING THE MIDDLE AGES it was customary to eat in the hall with the entire household, or in the bedroom *à deux*. The dining room did not evolve as a separate room until the 17th century, and even then it was not referred to specifically as a dining room, but as a parlour, a room that offered a degree of privacy, comfort and freedom from draughts and noise.

The first real country house dining room was at Houghton in Norfolk, a house designed by William Kent in 1732 in the rich Italianate style. It was situated on the *piano nobile* along with the other state entertaining rooms and therefore was not used on an everyday basis, but predominately when the owner, Sir Robert Walpole, was playing host to friends or

*BELOW The magnificent George III mahogany sideboard is veneered with satinwood. The wooden urn is a knife box, designed to keep table knives safe and sharp. Since Georgian knives were made of steel, they could be sharpened to a dangerous razor edge and had to be kept perfectly dry or rust would set in. The glass bonbonnière next to the knife box was filled with sweetmeats and passed around after dinner.*

*LEFT  Dining rooms were designed to look their best by night, sparkling with mahogany, silver and glass. These dramatic curtains were made to an original Regency design calling for gold fringing – substituted here with the more affordable lurex.*

*RIGHT  A fruitwood Hepplewhite-style shield-back dining chair.*

*BELOW  An original ormolu (gilded bronze) candle sconce provides additional light. On the side table is a set of Georgian blue glass decanters and glasses.*

*ABOVE A sideboard with a display of beautiful silver. Notice how the proportions of the painting and the delicacy of the frame relate to the dimensions of the piece of furniture beneath. The Georgians had a sharp eye for such detail.*

*FAR RIGHT The mahogany panelled door with its egg-and-dart moulding and the plaster over the door mantel are all new, but made to an original Georgian design. The walls above the dado rail are covered in a two-tone silk fabric that enhances the paintings.*

parliamentary colleagues. For everyday dining a less formal breakfast room or parlour was situated on the ground floor closer to the kitchens.

In grand country houses, where lavish entertaining had become an integral part of the fabric of life, a large dining room was essential, as the grand saloon, previously used for dining, was now given over to dancing. Eating and drinking occupied a large of the Georgians' day. The feasting typically began with a late breakfast around 10 a.m., followed by a light lunch at midday. The main meal of the day, dinner, was served mid-afternoon between 2 and 3 p.m., leaving the evenings free for visiting, dancing or games. By the mid-1700s it became fashionable to eat later, around 5 p.m., and this tradition persisted up to the Regency period in the early 19th century, when lunch became a more substantial meal and dinner was served in the evening between 7 and 8 p.m.

In houses with more than one eating room, breakfast was usually served in the less formal parlour. It was laid out on the sideboard as a buffet, and replenished throughout the morning for guests to come and help themselves as they pleased. Dinner was a formal occasion when guests changed into their evening gowns and a vast number of servants served huge quantities of meats, vegetables and fruits cultivated and produced, for the most part, on the estate.

When dining took place in parlours or grand saloons, it was normal practice for tables and chairs to be brought in by servants. Therefore many early Georgian dining chairs have simple, undecorated backs, as they would have been ranged up against the wall for much of the time. As the dining room

*BELOW  Sunlight and shadows play on the panelled walls of this country house dining room. A simple bouquet of fresh flowers from the garden brings in a breath of the outdoors.*

grew in importance, so the furniture required for dining evolved, and a large table, generally made from mahogany and surrounded by a matching set of chairs, became the focal point. In grander houses, pieces such as sideboards and mirrors were often designed by the architect and made by illustrious cabinet-makers to fit specific niches or walls in the dining room.

In small houses and terraced town houses, the eating room was less elaborately decorated than the drawing room, and frequently the panelling or wainscot was painted in bold, dark colours, unlike the earlier parlours which had wood-grained panelling or marbled walls. The dresser (a typical piece of parlour furniture) was removed to the kitchen and replaced

*BELOW The combination of silver, glass and china helps to create a grand sense of style in this early 19th-century dining room. The Pompeiian red walls provide a rich warm glow by night.*

*LEFT  A glorious profusion of late 18th-century plasterwork decorates the walls and ceiling of the grand dining room. The theme is distinctly neoclassical, with nymphs and cherubs ornamenting the characteristic ovals and medallions. Equally typical is the light touch of the delicate wreaths and intertwining festoons. The plasterwork contrasts with the heavy, early Georgian sideboards supported on the outstretched wings of eagles. The family crest appears on the polescreen and on the backs of the buttoned-leather dining chairs.*

generally made from mahogany to match the furniture. Mirrors, chandeliers and sconces were important elements in the decoration of the more formal dining room, as candlelight and reflected light played a vital part in setting the scene. Fireplaces were a necessity and the mantel shelf usually had a pair of lit candelabra in front of a mirror.

While drawing rooms were considered 'feminine', dining rooms were masculine enclaves. 'The eating rooms are considered as the apartments of conversation, in which we

[the men] are to pass a great part of our time,' wrote Robert Adam. It was traditional for country house dining rooms to have a suitably masculine sporting theme, reflected in the paintings and tapestries and the ornate plasterwork which often depicted animals and hunting horns. Bacchic ornament in the form of festoons of grapes and vines was another popular theme. To quote Robert Adam again, 'induced by the nature of our climate, we [in contrast to the French] indulge more largely in the enjoyment of the bottle'.

*ABOVE  Convex mirrors with built-in candle sconces are very efficient reflectors of light. They were introduced from France in the 1800s and soon became very fashionable in Georgian England. The plain marble fireplace is typically Regency in style, as are the dining table and chairs.*

## LIBRARIES AND STUDIES

FAR RIGHT *A magnificent library leading off a main entrance hall is seen through Georgian-style arches. The early Georgian chair in the foreground is as solid and comfortable to sit on as it is lovely to look at. It has the cabriole legs and ball-and-claw feet so typical of the period.*

BELOW *The drum table was a common feature in libraries. These tables were made to revolve so that books laid open on them could be admired by a group of people. This fine example is from the late 18th century.*

$I$N 18TH-CENTURY BRITAIN, printers began to produce beautiful books, rivalling for the first time those printed in continental Europe. Apart from standard works of scholarship, books were being produced with fine, hand-coloured, copper-plate or wood-engraved illustrations. Subjects covered included natural history, botany, history, architecture and topography. Books became collector's items as well as essential tools for the well-educated gentleman, and architects responded by including libraries in their house plans – one of the earliest being the library designed by William Kent at Houghton for Sir Robert Walpole. As a politician as well as an entrepreneur, he had a large and varied collection of books which were housed in a room next to his own quarters in built-in bookcases.

At first, the library was very much the gentleman's domain, a place where he could read and write in peace. Decoration tended toward the masculine, with dark colours and plenty of

wood. Mahogany was traditionally used for the bookcases and oak for the floor. Specific book-related furniture also developed: desks, library steps, desk chairs and reading stands, again mostly made of mahogany. Leather was used for desk tops, and chairs were upholstered in leather trimmed with brass-headed studs.

Gentlemen returned from their Grand Tours with packing cases filled with paintings, classical busts, clocks and maps, many of which found their way into the library. Globes, which had been produced since the 17th century, were also popular library pieces. They were often made as a pair, one showing the earth (terrestrial) and the other the heavens (celestial). Globes were mounted on mahogany stands designed to stand on the floor or on a desk.

*LEFT* Maps and globes were a Georgian passion. This 18th-century pull-down map of Dorset has been installed in front of a simple but practical run of bookshelves in a comfortable country house library.

*BELOW* This unusual and striking writing table, flanked by two armchairs with carved cabriole legs, forms a lovely composition.

*LEFT* Mahogany panelling, globes, leather-bound books and leather chairs were typical of the Georgian library.

*BELOW* A mid-Georgian side chair with a characteristic back is displayed next to a veneered secretaire with a glazed bookcase top. Georgian pens were made of sharpened quills — goose feathers were the most sought-after.

Gradually the library lost its male-only status and it became an area for family and guests to congregate and read or play games. In the late-Georgian and Regency era, additional pieces of furniture were made, such as games tables, free-standing bookcases and folio stands for maps and prints. Furnishings became less masculine and included comfortable seating, arranged congenially in the middle of the room or around the fireplace. Colours were lighter, the walls wallpapered, and bookcases painted white. Curtains were in chintz or lighter, coloured fabrics, and brightly coloured rugs were thrown over the wooden floors.

*BELOW If well cared for, leather-bound books should last several lifetimes. Bookshelves should be regularly dusted and the bindings kept supple with a proprietary leather dressing. Folding library steps are the most practical way to reach higher shelves.*

*LEFT AND BELOW* The mahogany bookshelves are edged with leather strips to protect the tops of the books. Open on the table below is the type of volume volume beloved by the Georgian library owner – a natural history book with exquisite hand-coloured plates.

## CORRIDORS AND LANDINGS

*ABOVE A pretty, semi-circular veneered commode with satinwood strips emphasising the simple lines. Pieces of furniture made to stand against walls inevitably had completely plain backs.*

*FAR RIGHT A ground-floor stone-flagged corridor with a Chippendale-style three-seater bench seat. The seat is flanked by fashionable Georgian urns, and the corridor is illuminated with simple hall lanterns.*

PALLADIAN ARCHITECTURE introduced the concept of the *enfilade* – where the main rooms of a house run in a sequence so one passes from one to the other without a corridor. But the idea never gained popularity in England, and the corridor was introduced as a way of reconciling the idea of a parade of rooms with a degree of privacy. In the early 18th century the corridor was something of a novelty. Sir John Vanbrugh, the architect of Blenheim Palace, was forced to explain to his client, the Duchess of Marlborough: 'The corridore Madame, is foreign, and signifies in plain English, no more than a passage.'

Passages were for servants to dash around the house unobtrusively with food, hot water, coal and candles. The grander concept of the corridor, it was soon discovered, could be ornamental as well as functional, offering long, dramatic vistas as well as routes of convenience.

RIGHT *Panelling on the door and doorcase indicates that this is the entrance to a principal bedroom. The mahogany double doors are another mark of importance. The Georgians were not afraid of colour – the landing walls are colour-washed a deep rose pink.*

BELOW *The upstairs landing of a small town house is lit by a lovely arched window which originally would have had no curtains. A collection of porcelain jugs is displayed on a pretty writing desk with elegant legs that echo the delicate lines of the balusters.*

## BEDROOMS AND BOUDOIRS

*ABOVE A Regency bedhead very much in the French 'Napoleonic' style. The ormolu appliqués of festoons, stars and cherubs are typical of Regency taste.*

IN MOST EARLY 18TH-CENTURY houses, the bedroom was situated on the *piano nobile* along with the other principal rooms. In a tradition stretching back to the 16th century, the bed was possibly the most important piece of furniture in the house – a result of an earlier form of entertaining, the *levée*, in which the most favoured guests were received in the inner sanctum, the bedchamber. By the second part of the century, this practice seemed distinctly old-fashioned. Privacy became desirable and the sleeping quarters concentrated on upper floors, separated from the entertaining rooms.

Early 18th-century beds were small and very high, making steps a necessity, but as the century progressed, beds became lower, lightweight fabrics such as silks, muslins and floral cottons replaced the heavier tapestries and damasks, and the posts became more delicate, often left exposed as curtaining was now used as decorative dressing rather than to draw shut and provide privacy.

Leading designers were still producing impressive beds in the prevailing fashion. Chinoiserie, which was the height of fashion from about 1740, was a popular choice for bedrooms. A classic example is at Nostell Priory, where Thomas

*ABOVE  The simple tallboy is typical of the bedroom furniture found in modest homes. Tallboy chests of drawers were made in two pieces so they could be manoeuvred up staircases.*

*LEFT, BELOW AND RIGHT* Three bedrooms that show how the Georgian style need not be kept pure, immaculate and completely authentic in every detail. The basic architecture welcomes the accretions of generations: accumulations of old chintz and embroidery, the mixture of fine mahogany furniture with the plain and simple pieces that have been cobbled together from a variety of sources. The term 'Georgian' suggests colour and comfort as well as elegance and exquisiteness. It is the bones of the English country house style and creates that cosy feeling of gently-faded grandeur.

Chippendale designed a roomful of exotic furniture to be used with the hand-painted Chinese wallpaper.

The dressing room was part of a suite of rooms occupying the *piano nobile,* more often than not the last room and therefore in the best position, on a corner. Early Georgian dressing rooms were ornately furnished, but small and private and known as cabinets or closets. If space allowed, both men and women had their own dressing rooms which were furnished accordingly: the gentleman's with dark, rich walls, the lady's in a light romantic style and furnished with workboxes and tea tables. Dressing rooms grew larger and more important as time went by and were used as rooms for entertaining intimate friends and attending to business matters. Gradually the dressing room lost its connection with the main bedroom, but remained on an upper floor. Decoration became more light-hearted, often reflecting fashionable tastes. The Print-Room look, with its engravings and *trompe l'oeil* frames, was particularly popular.

*BELOW Ladies' dressing tables and men's shaving tables were produced from the mid-18th century, usually in mahogany. It was customary for ornate dressing table sets to be displayed on these tables rather than hidden away in drawers and compartments. Later designs were influenced by French styles and a lighter look was achieved with paler woods such as satinwood or tulip wood decorated with inlay or marquetry.*

*RIGHT A guest bedroom with simply panelled walls and shutters. Georgian guest bedrooms were comfortable places since guests, who had probably taken several days over their journey, were expected to stay for months. Twin beds appeared in the mid-18th century under the guise of a health initiative — until then single beds were a rarity, and the idea of sleeping apart yet in the same room was quite new.*

One of the most essential pieces of Georgian bedroom or dressing room furniture was the night commode or pot cuboard, which discreetly concealed a simple earthenware or porcelain chamber pot. In modest bedrooms they looked like wooden boxes, but in grander bedrooms they were disguised as chests of drawers. Baths were seldom taken, and when they were, it was in a hip bath filled with hot water brought up from the kitchen by the servants. For everyday washing, the washstand was devised to hold a basin and a ewer, and gentlemen had their specialized shaving stands.

*BELOW   A Regency mahogany dressing stand with an inset porcelain bowl, designed for use in a gentleman's dressing room. On the deep sill stands a George III oval dressing mirror with its original glass, and a chamber candlestick for lighting the way up the stairs to bed.*

*LEFT AND BELOW The walls are hung with a hand-painted silk after the design of a Georgian oriental wallpaper. It was considered inauspicious to cut through a bird or animal, so it was an essential skill of the paperhanger to overlap animal figures over the joins.*

BELOW *A restrained early 19th-century look for a single bedroom with muslin drapery over an ironwork canopy. The drapes and loops and the soft palette of colours are very Regency in style.*

RIGHT *A riot of* Toile de Jouy, *a printed fabric depicting rural scenes that was introduced from France in the mid-18th century. The mantel mirror and the day bed are typical Regency pieces.*

## DOORS

THE GEORGIAN DOOR is characterized by its panels, with the size, style and finish varying throughout the period depending on the grandeur or simplicity of the house and the location of the door. Early Georgian doors were elegantly tall and typically had six or eight fielded, or raised, panels which sometimes complemented the design of the cornice plasterwork, with egg-and-dart moulding among the most popular. Main rooms were often entered through double

doors set into deep reveals, and the higher in up the house, the simpler the doors became. Principal doors were often of polished mahogany, but architraves were generally painted. The doorcases of principal rooms received a lot of attention and many were decorated with painted or plaster reliefs in the panel above the door. Early doors were usually topped with a pediment, sometimes an open pediment incorporating a vase or bust. Door furniture consisted of elegant brass drop handles or doorknobs, which became more ornate as the period progressed.

In the mid-18th century, rococo themes were reflected in the plasterwork and architraving, and door furniture became more elaborate and prolific. Finger plates were introduced and escutcheons replaced rim locks.

Late Georgian neoclassical details included mouldings and carvings in contrast woods such as ebony, and painted doors were picked out in a variety of shades to enhance the panelling. Friezes were decorated with neoclassical motifs, typically garlands or festoons with bucrania (skull masks) and anthemions, or any of the many variations devised by the designers of the period. By the 1780s, curved doors had been developed to fit the fashion for oval rooms.

Regency style reverted to simple lines with columns and architraves following the classical Greek revival. Double doors were still popular, but with a simple architrave and flat panels, maybe emphasized in a contrast wood. Wood-grain paint effects and china doorknobs date from this period.

*LEFT Mahogany double doors set in a deep, panelled doorcase signify the entrance to the main room used for entertaining. The ebony doorknobs and escutcheons are original; the brass finger plates, a later addition, are adorned with Pegasus, the winged horse of classical mythology, associated with the Muses and the spring of inspiration.*

*BELOW LEFT AND RIGHT Two examples of brass door furniture. The design on the left is a lovely example of a circular patera with a beaded surround. The doorknob below has a gadrooned, or lobed finish. Antique door furniture can be bought from architectural salvage specialists, but some companies make new pieces to Georgian designs.*

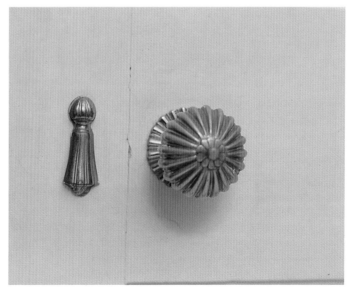

## WALLS AND CEILINGS

I N MOST EARLY Georgian houses, walls in the smarter rooms were panelled and divided into three: the field, dado and cornice. The wood used was deal (pine or fir), painted with a flat finish and sometimes picked out in other shades or with gilding. Later, wainscot panelling was used below the dado, and the walls above were plastered and either painted or wallpapered. Sheets of wallpaper were small and were hung as panels, fixed with a moulding or wooden fillet. Fabrics were stretched over battens and finished with a trim.

*BELOW Detail of a Georgian panelled room and doorway, typical of even quite modest houses. The play of light and shade created by the mouldings and panels accentuate the proportions of the room.*

*RIGHT In contrast to the simple panelling below, the panels here are elaborate and complex. The fluted pilaster decorating the doorcase can be seen on the left and the finely carved decoration in the architrave is gilded.*

*LEFT Detail of a pillared hall. Pillars were made of wood, stone or marble, and wooden ones were often painted to look like marble if the owner could not afford the real thing.*

Decorative plasterwork was sometimes found in the main entertaining rooms, in the hall and staircase, generally painted in a plain colour, usually white. It was not until Adam's time that colour was used to enhance plasterwork — earlier architects preferred the natural highlighting effects of light and shadow. Ceilings of early Georgian houses were plastered, nearly always with a moulding or cornice, the grandeur of the room dictating the amount of money spent on the ceiling. The grandest early Georgian homes made use of vaulted ceilings on staircases and in halls, with coffering to give them a heavy and serious look.

*ABOVE Reeded moulding was particularly fashionable from the end of the 18th century and into the first half of the 19th. Here, arch and ceiling mouldings are decorated with simple roundels.*

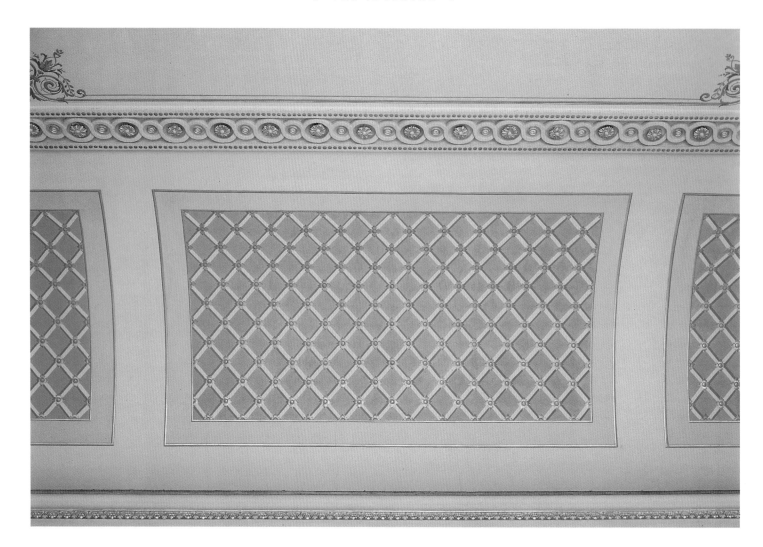

*ABOVE AND RIGHT* This delicate and elaborate gilded moulding includes lattice with rosettes on the overlap, paterae, beading and egg-and-dart motifs. The traditional method of gilding was to paint the ground with an oil-based size before applying thin sheets of gold or silver leaf.

TOP, LEFT AND ABOVE *Details of typical Georgian interior moulding on a doorcase, skirting, and dado (respectively). The degree of decoration is in direct relation to the importance of the room. The shell flanked by scrolling foliage is typical of the first half of the 18th century, as is the egg-and-dart moulding on the pediment.*

*LEFT Stairwells were frequently lit from above by a cupola – a circular or oval window in the roof. The shape of the window might be echoed by a pattern on the floor in stone or marble.*

Later Georgian houses ousted panelling below the dado in favour of plaster and paint in a contrast colour or a *faux* finish emulating marble or wood grain. Above the dado, walls were still adorned with silks and velvets, and colours such as yellow, turquoise and deep coral pinks became popular. Cornices and plasterwork became more elaborate with swags and ribbons and acanthus leaves and, under Robert Adam's influence, motifs on Etruscan and Roman themes. Gothick details were popular too, lasting into the Regency period. In general ceilings were left relatively plain, with just a cornice and a ceiling rose.

During the Regency period, walls were still broken up according to the rules of proportion, but were generally wallpapered above the dado. Striped papers were very fashionable. Dark colours were used in halls and dining rooms, and special paint effects such as marbleising, wood-graining and *trompe l'oeil* effects such as tented ceilings and drapery over doorways gained popularity. Ceilings, although less elaborately decorated, were treated with architectural emphasis on shape and form.

*ABOVE This ceiling has a Jacobean flavour. The Regency period, from which this ceiling dates, was an eclectic one and many periods and styles were plundered for decoration.*

## MOULDINGS AND PANELLING

PANELLING AND DECORATIVE mouldings played a large part in defining the Georgian look. They were both practical and decorative, concealing joins and changes of level while visually defining the proportions of a wall or door along the lines of the classical Orders and forming a harmonious transition from one element to the next. It was the style and the complexity of the detail that followed the vagaries of fashion, not the position or function of the moulding. Simple rooms might just have a plain, curved moulding; the more important and impressive designs were taken from the Palladian pattern books.

Early mouldings needed to be fairly substantial, as they often had a structural job to do. The bolection moulding, for

*LEFT Window shutters were made of hinged panels that folded back on themselves and fitted into recesses within the reveal. These shutters, with their delicate ironwork pull handles are enriched with the ubiquitous egg-and-dart moulding.*

*BELOW Most Georgian windows were fitted with shutters which were closed at night for added warmth and perhaps for security. In true Georgian style these would be panelled too — the proportions of the shutter panels carefully aligned with the glazing bars.*

*ABOVE  The moulding just below the windowsill is a Vitruvian, or wavescroll, a pattern found in Greek and Roman cultures. It was a common border ornament for architectural detail and for silverware in the 18th century.*

instance, was a convex moulding specifically devised to disguise and elaborate joins between surfaces of uneven levels. At this stage, mouldings and panelling were made of wood, panels were flat, usually painted, with no applied mouldings and were divided by a series of stiles and rails.

As building techniques progressed, along with the fashion for more elaborate decoration, fielded, or raised, panels were introduced, often edged with a moulding such as the popular egg-and-dart moulding, known to the Georgians through the works of Palladio.

It was customary for a moulding detail to be repeated throughout a room, obviously to different scales and with variations to the theme. In grander houses, in order to ensure

*ABOVE AND RIGHT  Such was the care and skill put into Georgian buildings that even glazing bars were given a decorative profile, providing yet further opportunity for craftsmen and carpenters to display their talents.*

*LEFT  In this Regency dining room, the woodwork has been restored to its original state and ebonized, with the moulding picked out with gilding. Ebonized and very dark woods were highly fashionable in the early years of the 19th century.*

continuity, the architect designed every detail from the pattern on the cornice to the door architrave and the fireplaces, but in smaller houses, standard designs were taken from pattern books. Early Georgian mouldings were solid and raised, as they were carved from wood. By the neoclassical period at the end of the century, the development of plaster-casting techniques meant that more delicate effects could be achieved. Mouldings consequently became much flatter and more delicate, and the designs followed complex Greek forms such as the anthemions, palmettes and groups of figures made popular by the Adam brothers. Light, waterproof papier-mâché decorations became a popular option for ready-made wall and ceiling ornament in the Regency period.

Panelling went from crude and simple, to highly decorative, and then returned to a refined simplicity. Fine reeding and simple beading were used as discreet finishing details for many areas such as fireplaces and door surrounds, and these simple, elegant lines continued in popularity well into the Regency years.

*ABOVE LEFT  These shutters have a soft, chalky, dragged painted finish, achieved using several shades of off-white. Bright, shiny whites were unknown in Georgian times, and if used today would destroy the delicate colour balance of a period interior.*

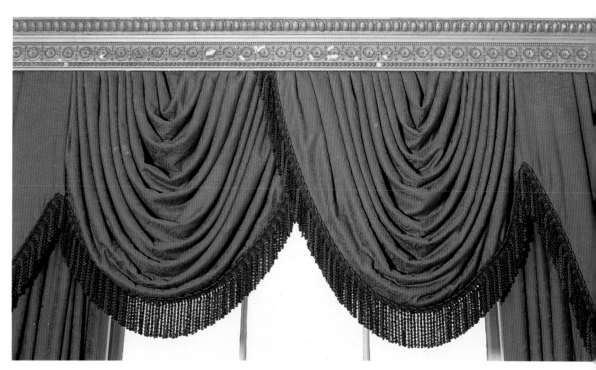

## PELMETS AND DRAPES

Curtains were found on beds long before they were used on windows. The average early Georgian house had no curtains; most windows were fitted with shutters which helped retain heat and keep out sunlight. If curtains existed they were simple pieces of wool or hessian cloth with loops across the top, hanging on a rod. Roller blinds, patented by William Bayley in 1692, were used to protect furnishings from direct sunlight. By the 1730s curtains came in pairs, and in the homes of the rich, expensive imported fabrics were being used. Mid-way through the century, curtains had become an essential decorative item.

Festoon curtains, made from a lightweight fabric such as silk, were common in the mid-1700s, their advantage being that they took up little space and did not obscure the architrave. Later curtains came in pairs with fringes, ropes, tassels and braids used to enhance the treatments. Pelmets were introduced largely to hide the curtain rods, but also as a further decorative touch. Carved and gilded pelmets were reserved for grander houses and were often designed to match plaster cornices.

It was during the Regency period that window treatments were at their most elaborate, influenced by the French fashion for draping fabric everywhere.

*ABOVE AND FAR LEFT A gilded curtain cornice with applied plasterwork decorations of beading, gadrooning and rosettes provides a head for elaborate drapery. Fringed swags and tails were features of the Regency period, as were full-length curtains to dress the newly-fashionable french windows. Rich, heavy red curtains were the traditional choice for the libraries and dining rooms.*

## FLOORS

IN COUNTRY COTTAGES and the ground-level floors of town houses, floors were originally made of compressed earth. In the early Georgian era this gave way to brick, clay or stuccoed floors. The stucco, made from plaster and coloured with animal blood, was either left natural or, as fashions changed, mixed with aggregates and painted to look like stone, marble or wood.

In grand houses, stone floors were considered a status symbol for entrance halls and saloons. Whole floors of marble slabs were used in the great houses in entrance halls and ground-floor reception rooms. Different colours of marble were used to create complicated geometric patterns.

Early Georgian wooden floors were made of oak. The boards were linked together with dowels and nailed into the joists below. The hand-made boards tended to be wide, up to 12 inches or more, and constant scrubbing with water and sand bleached the untreated boards to a soft gold colour.

Towards the mid-18th century, pine and fir replaced oak, which was by then in short supply. Boards were stained and polished or limed and painted to look like stone. Parquetry

*FAR LEFT AND BELOW Two stone floors that demonstrate the level of care lavished on every detail. Although the squares have been laid diagonally to give visual width to the rooms, there are carefully considered borders at the edges and on the threshold of the drawing room (below). The decorative inset squares of dark marble or slate are typical of the Georgian hall.*

floors were not very popular after the mid-18th century, but they came back into fashion in the 1800s thanks to the French taste for more elaborate designs. Varnish was used to protect wooden floors, and rugs were found in all rooms. Robert Adam encouraged a fashion for elaborate flooring, his designs for stone or marble inlays and for woven carpets frequently reflected the plasterwork on the ceiling.

Carpets were first made at Wilton, in Wiltshire in the 1740s. The carpet came in strips which were sewn together to fit the floor, perhaps with an added, decorative border. Entrance halls were rarely carpeted, but during the Regency period it was common to use narrow 'turkey' carpets on wooden staircases. For more modest rooms, carpets consisted of simple floorcloths, which were also used to protect the fine carpets of grand homes from wear and dirt.

*RIGHT   Unpretentious stone flags were typically used for service areas, sculleries and kitchens throughout the Georgian era. They were laid straight onto compressed earth and were consequently rather damp underfoot. Brick pavoirs were another common option for these domestic areas.*

*RIGHT   In stunning contrast, a beautifully laid marble floor. Marble was the most expensive flooring option, but a fashionable one throughout the 18th century. Inigo Jones, known as the 'godfather of Palladianism' introduced marble floors to England in 1616, when he built the Queen's House in Greenwich.*

## STAIRS AND BANISTERS

ABOVE An unusual combination of wood and ironwork balusters on the same staircase. The tread ends are decorated with carved wooden paterae. Stair carpets were a late Georgian innovation. John Loudon, who wrote on furnishing the average house, stated: 'Stair carpets give an air of great comfort and finish to a house. No cottage should be without one.'

THE STAIRCASE was an important architectural feature in the early Georgian home, and many houses had two: a main one leading off the entrance hall or from an adjacent inner lobby, and a back staircase, reserved for servants, running from basement to attic. Early staircases were made of wood either with a closed string at the side hiding the treads or an open string to show off the carved tread ends. Balusters were fixed to the treads, at a ratio of two or three balusters per tread. The main floors had elaborately turned and carved balusters which became simpler as the staircase rose or descended. Early balusters of oak or mahogany were chunky

RIGHT Three examples of the extraordinary variety in a feature as simple as a newel post. In general, the complex woodturning of early Georgian balusters gradually gave way to ironwork. The exquisite inlaid flourish on the curve of the rail (above, far right) is a beautiful reminder of an age when craftsmanship reigned supreme.

in design, often straight with a simple square block-and-urn design, and usually polished. Pine balusters were painted, but the banister rail was always polished. Then a slim, straight baluster became fashionable, and those who could afford it chose balusters delicately worked in iron.

In grander houses with stone staircases, balusters were made of ironwork and steel with designs reflecting details typical of the mid-to late-Georgian period, such as rococo scrollwork or neoclassical lyres. The ironwork was usually painted black with details picked out in gilt. Towards the end of the century balusters became simpler, and more importance was given to the newel post and the shape of the tread ends. Metal balusters were common in all but the most modest of houses by the Regency period, as many of the designs were standard and made from cast iron with classical motifs. A spectacular example of the non-standard staircase can be found in the Royal Pavilion, Brighton, a chinoiserie delight made of cast iron and simulated bamboo.

*FAR LEFT AND ABOVE LEFT These two staircases demonstrate the technical virtuosity of the late 18th and early 19th centuries. The shallow rise and slim stone treads (far left) seem to float in space with no means of support. This was the result of the development of the iron frame and cantilever technique which Regency housebuilders exploited to the maximum.*

## FIREPLACES

Basic designs changed very little over the century – it was the carvings, mouldings and materials that changed. Early fireplaces were simple and made of wood to match the panelled walls. The interior was made of brick with an iron fire back and a dog grate on which to place logs. Once coal became common, small raised coal grates replaced the dogs.

Grand Georgian rooms had fireplaces of ornately carved marble or stone that reflected the style of the room. Correct proportions were paramount and were determined by the height of the ceiling, the width of the walls and the dictates of the latest pattern book.

Design simplified during the neoclassical period and decoration was elegantly restrained, but fireplaces in the main rooms remained status symbols to the eye of the connoisseur, as the simple structure was often made from rare, imported, coloured marbles. Moving into the Regency period, fireplaces became smaller in order to function better.

*LEFT  A masterpiece of a fireplace and overmantel conceived as one design, together with a charming portrait of the original lady of the house fashionably dressed up à la bergère.*

*BELOW LEFT  The depth and detail of the woodcarving on this fireplace is extraordinarily fine. The festoons, scrolling foliage and garlands all speak of abundance and wealth.*

*RIGHT  A frieze of nymphs runs along the top of this Adam-inspired marble fireplace. The pink marble inset is original, but the brick infill and enclosed grate are later additions.*

*BELOW An Adam-style fireplace with Ionic column detail and a central panel depicting an idealized goatherd playing the pipes to his flock. The grate surround is of steel and brass.*

*LEFT   A grand, stone Palladian chimneypiece with its original, open log grate. The central lion mask is a typical early 18th-century naturalistic depiction of this popular symbol of courage, pride and majesty.*

*BELOW   A restrained Regency-style fireplace with a coal-burning grate. Black marble was traditionally used for dining rooms, white for drawing rooms.*

# FOUR

# DESIGN
# DIRECTORY

RBITERS OF STYLE in the Georgian and Regency

eras did not necessarily create designs

themselves. What they had in common was

a realization that a vast audience for visual information

on the latest styles and motifs existed, and they met this

need by publishing pattern books. Although some of

these pattern books were relatively expensive

productions, it is likely that each copy had a wide

circulation among the patrons, clients, builders and

craftsmen of the day.

# ANDREA PALLADIO
## 1508 – 1580

AN ITALIAN ARCHITECT, who trained as a stonemason and sculptor, Palladio's influence through his published works and subsequent editions of them, was so important that Palladianism became an architectural term in its own right and defined the prevalent style in Georgian Britain for the first half of the 18th century, and well into the second.

Palladio provided a clear reference for the Renaissance and subsequent years of the structure and ornament of classical Roman architecture. His book, *I Quattro Libri dell'Architettura,* published in Venice in 1570, was partly based on the only writing on architecture to survive from classical antiquity, Vitruvius's *De Architectura.* Vitruvius provided the key to using the classical orders, and an explanation of the proportion and symmetry of early Roman architecture complete with rules of measurement. Palladio's book had clear visual illustrations and was thus invaluable to builders and craftsmen, not only to his contemporaries, but also for the next two centuries thanks to the number of translations and editions of the book that proliferated during these years.

Besides the orders, Palladio included drawings and plans for domestic buildings, not only Roman examples, but also buildings of his own design, and for bridges and temples, which were invaluable for the ornamentation of the great 18th- century parks. He also produced, in great detail, schemes of interior and exterior ornamentation.

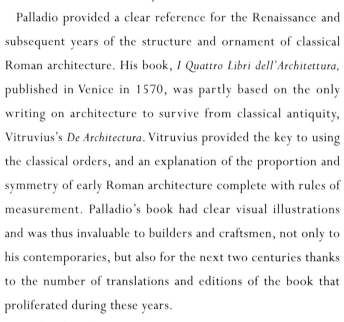

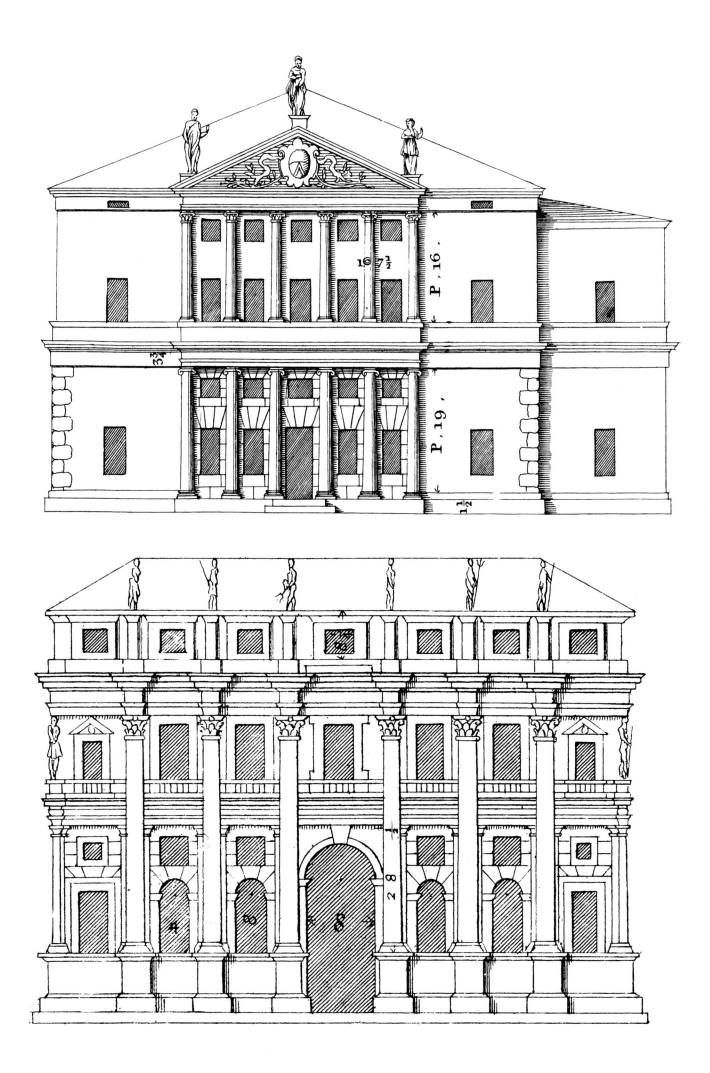

# BATTY LANGLEY
## 1696 – 1751

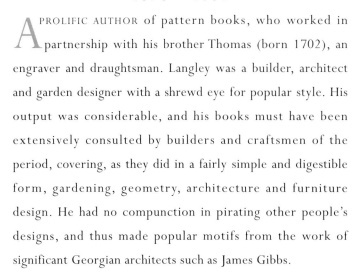

A PROLIFIC AUTHOR of pattern books, who worked in partnership with his brother Thomas (born 1702), an engraver and draughtsman. Langley was a builder, architect and garden designer with a shrewd eye for popular style. His output was considerable, and his books must have been extensively consulted by builders and craftsmen of the period, covering, as they did in a fairly simple and digestible form, gardening, geometry, architecture and furniture design. He had no compunction in pirating other people's designs, and thus made popular motifs from the work of significant Georgian architects such as James Gibbs.

His earliest work was *Practical Geometry,* published in 1726 and his most popular was *The City and Country Builder's and Workman's Treasury of Designs,* which although first published in 1740 went into numerous subsequent editions, and included some up-to-the-minute rococo designs which he copied from French and German designers. Batty Langley's name is most associated with the whimsical gothick style so popular in the mid-18th century, and these illustrations all come from *Gothic Architecture* of 1747, which was a reworking of an earlier collection of designs, *Ancient Architecture restored and improved by rules and proportions in many grand designs of columns, doors, windows,* published in 1742. He devised a controversial set of five new orders of architecture in the gothick style, which did not catch on; however his placing of gothick motifs, such as trefoils, quatrefoils, crockets and the ubiquitous pointed arch was influential and appeared on countless garden temples, fireplaces, windows and porches throughout the country.

# THOMAS CHIPPENDALE
## 1718 – 1779

THOMAS CHIPPENDALE IS the most celebrated name in English furniture design. A practising cabinet-maker, whose workshop produced some of the finest quality furniture of his day, he also published in 1754 the first important book of furniture patterns: *The Gentleman and Cabinet-Maker's Director,* a folio volume containing 160 engraved plates, which ran to three editions. Although originally intended as an advertisement for his own firm, its influence was extraordinarily wide-ranging. Copies were owned by 18th-century architects, cabinet-makers, wood-carvers, joiners, plasterers and founders, who made free use of his designs which included, most famously, his chairs, but also sideboards, dressing chests, cabinets, sofas and desks.

Chippendale's *Director* offered what he described as designs in 'the Gothic, Chinese and Modern Taste'. By 'modern taste' he meant rococo – a style that became generally popular during the middle years of the century. Since it had originated in France, the British craftsmen needed guidance on how to master the complex scrollwork and asymmetry and how to apply the ornament to furniture. Chippendale employed two other designers, Matthias Lock and Henry Copland, who were familiar with the idiom, to come up with designs on his behalf. His work is particularly associated with chinoiserie and his Chinese-style fretwork and lattice designs were very popular. Accompanying each plate was advice for the suitability of the design – for example, he recommended that his Chinese Chairs were 'very popular for a Lady's Dressing-Room: especially if it is hung with India paper'.

# ROBERT ADAM 1728 – 1792
# & JAMES ADAM 1732 – 1794

ROBERT ADAM WAS THE MOST brilliant of the three architect brothers (the third being John 1721–1792) whose designs for buildings, interiors and objects set the style for much of the last half of the 18th century. In the 1750s he travelled in Rome and Dalmatia, studying classical antiquities first hand. On his return he and his brothers set up as architects and rapidly came to prominence. *The Works in Architecture* of Robert and James Adam was published in instalments between 1773 and 1779 and was vastly influential in disseminating their style, which introduced a new lightness and elegance to Georgian houses.

*The Works* recorded the principal buildings they had worked on, but more importantly, the interiors, furniture and fittings they had designed which, taken together, made a cohesive style. Rejecting the heavier Palladian ornament and the excesses of rococo, the Adam brothers offered, in their own words: 'a beautiful variety of light mouldings, gracefully formed, delicately enriched and arranged with propriety and skill'. Many of their trademark motifs were adapted from their particular study of the newly excavated wall-paintings of Pompeii and Herculaneum, such as griffons, swags of bellflowers, medallions and dancing nymphs. Other favourite motifs – anthemions, palmettes, sphinxes and urns – were adapted from the 'Etruscan' Greek black and red vases, which were being excavated and collected in large numbers.

Design of the Ceiling of the Library or Great Room, at Kenwood.

Dessein du Plafond de la Bibliotheque de la Villa de Kenwood.

# GEORGE HEPPLEWHITE
## D. 1786

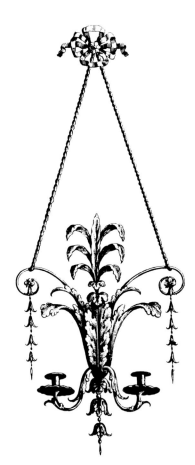

ALTHOUGH HEPPLEWHITE IS well known as a name associated with Georgian furniture design, very little is known about his life. His reputation is entirely based on a collection of 300 designs for household furniture which were published two years after his death as *The Cabinet-Maker and Upholsterer's Guide.* The first edition of 1788 was followed by two subsequent editions issued under the name of his widow Alice in 1789 and 1794.

The style of the designs is elegantly neoclassical, with the ornamentation of festoons, medallions, rosettes, vases and paterae owing much to the style of the Adam brothers. He addressed the design of a large number of furnishings in great detail, ranging from bow-fronted chests-of-drawers, wardrobes and beds, to a wide number of smaller items such as wall brackets, firescreens, tea trays, lamps, pedestals and vases. His name is particularly associated with oval and shield-backed chairs and a design which incorporated the Prince of Wales's feathers as a decorative motif. The fashion at this period was for lighter-coloured woods and finishes, and Hepplewhite's patterns for chair backs and table tops could be carried out either in satinwood veneer or painted, as some of his notes on his chair designs reveal: 'When japanned or painted to harmonize with the colour scheme of the room, a lighter framework than that requisite for mahogany is permissable. This type should have cane bottoms, with cushions covered with linen or cotton cases to accord with general hue of chair. Medallions, printed or painted on silk, are frequently inserted in the circular motives'.

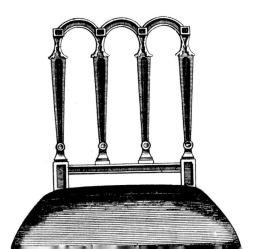

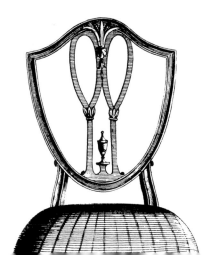

# THOMAS SHERATON
## 1751 — 1806

THOMAS SHERATON IS THE THIRD in the triumvirate (with Chippendale and Hepplewhite), whose names, by virtue of their published pattern books, are irrevocably associated with Georgian furniture design. Although Sheraton did practice as a cabinet-maker he never had his own workshop and was a writer and teacher of drawing and geometry, as well as a Baptist minister and bookseller.

Sheraton's most famous book is *The Cabinet-Maker and Upholsterer's Drawing-Book*, published in 1793. Three further editions were published before 1802, it was translated into German and was extremely influential in America among the Federal-style designers. In this book Sheraton collected together a range of furniture that he saw as the best and most representative of current London fashion. It therefore provided a lead to cabinet-makers throughout the provinces whose work was, in the main, for a growing middle-class clientele. His designs have two characteristic lines: on the one hand, a pretty, rather feminine style characterized by serpentine curves and bow fronts ornamented with light-coloured veneers and painted decoration continuing the tradition of Adam; on the other a more austere neoclassical approach with clean lines and a more subdued ornamentation such as reeding and geometric panels. This was the forerunner of much that found favour in the fully-blown Regency style which he explored more fully in his last two books: *The Cabinet Dictionary* of 1803 and *The Cabinet-Maker, Upholsterer, and General Artist's Encyclopaedia* of 1804–1807.

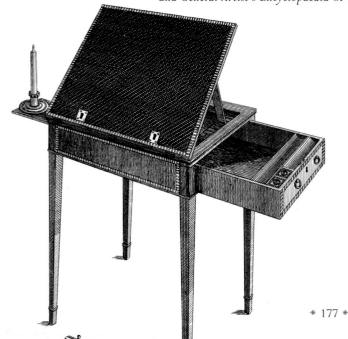

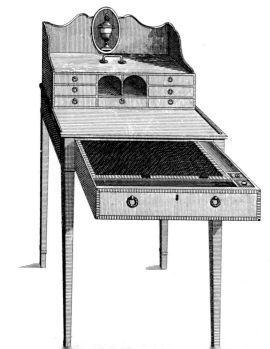

# THOMAS HOPE
## 1769 – 1831

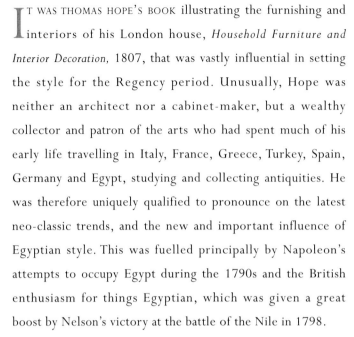

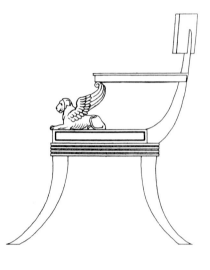

I T WAS THOMAS HOPE'S BOOK illustrating the furnishing and interiors of his London house, *Household Furniture and Interior Decoration,* 1807, that was vastly influential in setting the style for the Regency period. Unusually, Hope was neither an architect nor a cabinet-maker, but a wealthy collector and patron of the arts who had spent much of his early life travelling in Italy, France, Greece, Turkey, Spain, Germany and Egypt, studying and collecting antiquities. He was therefore uniquely qualified to pronounce on the latest neo-classic trends, and the new and important influence of Egyptian style. This was fuelled principally by Napoleon's attempts to occupy Egypt during the 1790s and the British enthusiasm for things Egyptian, which was given a great boost by Nelson's victory at the battle of the Nile in 1798.

Hope bought his house in Duchess Street in 1799 and created spectacular interiors to display his collection of Greek, Roman and Egyptian antiquities. He furnished the house with careful reconstructions of ancient furniture. One of his extensively imitated precepts was that ornament should always be appropriate to the purpose of the room or object. A dining room and its furnishings should therefore be emblematic of Bacchus, the god of wine, and Ceres, goddess of agriculture; and a library must make allusions to Minerva, goddess of wisdom.

Other hallmarks of his style included lavish use of animal masks and feet, tripod forms, lyre-shaped supports and furniture with cross-frames and sabre-shaped legs. Hope produced all the original drawings for *Household Furniture* himself, and followed it with a volume entitled *Costume of the Ancients* in 1809.

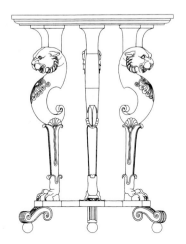

# RUDOLPH ACKERMANN
## 1764 — 1834

ACKERMANN WAS A book and print-seller, publisher and art supplier whose monthly magazine *The Repository of Arts, Literature, Commerce, Manufacture, Fashions and Politics* provided, as no regular publication had done before in Britain, an up-to-date summary of prevailing taste. It ran from 1809 to 1828. Apart from news both political and financial, Ackermann included coloured plates, not only of latest architectural developments in London and the country, but also of 'Fashionable Furniture'.

These illustrations included individual pieces of furniture and fireplaces and decorative schemes for rooms including window treatments, which showed in detail the full complexity of Regency curtains with their muslin sub-curtains, draperies, valances and ornamented curtain rods. In its heyday *The Repository* was selling about 2,000 copies a month, and it is easy to surmise that many people, both patrons and craftsmen, must have perused its attractive colour illustrations for news of the latest designs. Ackermann provided patterns in the new Greek revival style, the latest from France (once Napoleon was safely defeated), and finally in the Gothic Revival style, which was rather more subdued than its mid-18th-century rococo predecessor, the gothick.

## HUMPHRY REPTON
### 1752 – 1818

AFTER STARTING HIS CAREER as a Norfolk cloth merchant, Humphry Repton launched himself as a landscape gardener – he was the first person to use the term – at the end of the 1780s. He was immediately successful and gained a wide range of clients who employed him to create, within their parkland, picturesque settings to enhance their country houses. Repton was not didactic, and convinced his clients that gardens were essentially for use and enjoyment: 'Convenience ought to take the lead in a constant residence, since picturesque effect is too dearly bought at the price of comfort'.

Repton considered the house and garden as an entity, and provided a design in which each complemented the other. For example, while he realized that many of his clients might need or wish to have stock in surrounding fields or land, he

was insistent that any fencing should be as unobtrusive as possible and not spoil lines of vision. He therefore made much use of the ha-ha and recommended that fences be painted 'dark, or as it is called, an invisible green'.

Repton's notions were also applicable to small villas and even cottages, since Regency architecture was very concerned with the flow between garden and house. This was the period of french and floor-length windows and Repton showed how terraces, pergolas and flower gardens might be laid out to surround the house, providing an extension of the interior style. He provided individual 'Red Books' for clients, which showed by a use of flaps and overlays how the garden and park would look before and after his designs had been carried out. He also provided designs for small temples and seats. For general circulation, but using the same principle, he published *Observations on the Theory and Practice of Landscape Gardening* in 1805.

## PAINTS

S O MUCH TIME AND EFFORT went into the valued work of carpenters and joiners, both on the exterior and in the interior of the Georgian home, that the protection of woodwork was paramount. Paint was, of course, the first line of defence. Oil paints were based on white lead with the addition of natural pigment. Evidence shows that these paints were not glossy, but had a matt finish, achieved with the addition of turpentine.

Distemper, a water-based paint, was used on plastered walls. The wonderfully soft, powdery finish of distemper, made by binding pigment with a form of milk whey strengthened with linseed oil, was not washable, but it breathed well and was particularly suitable for damp walls.

'Invisible green' and stone colours were used for exterior joinery. Pale colours were used for service rooms and passageways (bright whites are a 20th-century invention), reds and pinks were considered appropriate for living rooms, greys, blues and greens for the bedchambers.

*BELOW AND FAR RIGHT   All paints are from The Historic Colours range by Fired Earth. They are representative of the earth pigments in use prior to 1820.*

| Gypsum | Roman ochre | Stone ochre |
| --- | --- | --- |
| Yellow drab | Oxford ochre | Sienna earth |

Bistre

Sandarac

Mummy

Pompeian red

Better Class red

Dragon's blood red

Mineral grey

Verdigris

Invisible green

Terre vert

Ultramarine ashes

Blue verditer

## WALLPAPER

WALLPAPER BECAME FASHIONABLE from the 1740s onwards, replacing panelling above the dado rail. The first wallpaper factory in Britain was set up by John Baptist Jackson in the 1740s, who published a book on the subject in 1756, describing how the patterns were printed using woodblocks. Although he did try oil colour, it was distemper paint that proved the most successful. Technology soon improved and paper was printed from copperplates off rollers, and then hand-coloured. There was a large variety of patterns available from quite an early period; ranging from stripes with sprigs of flowers, to architectural motifs such as neoclassical niches and gothick arches as well as papers that imitated stonework, marble, scagliola and tiling.

Tradecards from 18th-century wallpaper suppliers show that they called themselves paper stainers; one ' Matthew Darly on the Strand' at his ' Manufactory for Paper Hangings' offered 'Cielings, Pannels, Staircases, Chimney Boards etc. Neatly fitted up either with Paintings or Stainings in the Modern, Gothic or Chinese Taste for Town or Country'.

*LEFT* Temple Newsom *c. 1820.* *RIGHT* *Clockwise from centre:* Shepherd and Sheep *c. 1760, used at Doddington Hall;* Clandon, *a late 18th-century design;* Regency, *a hand-blocked paper;* Bamboo trellis, *c. 1815 used in Brighton Pavillion;* Large Anthemium border, *early 19th century;* Alma Trellis, *early 19th century; and* Regency bracket. *All wallpapers by Cole & Son.*

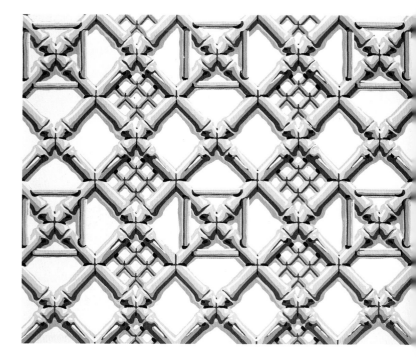

# GLOSSARY

ACANTHUS LEAF  Foliage ornament based on the heavy, drooping leaves of the acanthus plant.

ADAM STYLE  In the style of the Scottish architect Robert Adam and his brothers, heavily influenced by Roman, Greek and especially Pompeiian motifs.

ANTHEMIONS  Repeating floral ornament frequently used on friezes and cornices.

ARCHITRAVE  Moulding around a door or window frame.

BACCHIC ORNAMENT  Decoration related to the god Bacchus and thus to wine and wine drinking, such as festoons of grapes and vines.

BALUSTERS  Individual vertical forms that make up a balustrade. Found on staircases, balconies and parapets.

BAROQUE  A variant of classicism, characterised by elaborate ornamentation. A style of sculptural, curving forms.

BARREL VAULT  A vaulted ceiling in the shape of a half cylinder.

BEVELLED EDGE  An angled edge, usually of mirror glass.

BOLECTION MOULDING  Convex moulding used to disguise and elaborate the join between two unequal levels.

BOUDOIR  A woman's dressing room or private sitting room. From the French *bouder,* to sulk.

BROKEN PEDIMENT  A pediment broken at the base of the triangle. *see:* pediment; open pediment.

BUCRANIUM  The skull of a ram, ox, bull or goat in Graeco-Roman classical ornament.

CABRIOLE LEG  Ornamental curving leg used on furniture.

CARTOUCHE  A framed, decorative panel.

CHIMERA  A creature from classic mythology that breathes fire composed of the head of a lion, the body of a goat and the wings of an eagle.

CHINOISERIE  A decorative style inspired by the Orient, and very popular in the 18th century as it offered an alternative to the principles of symmetry.

COFFERING  Recessed panels, usually ornamented, sunk into a ceiling or dome to form an overall pattern.

COMPOSITE ORDER  Composed of elements of the Ionic and Corinthian Orders. Viewed by purists as fit only for theatrical scenery and not to be taken at all seriously.

CONSOLE TABLE  A table supported against a wall on 'console' or scrolled legs.

CORINTHIAN ORDER  *see:* Orders. The most ornamental and elaborate of the Orders, generally used on a small scale.

CORNICE  Ornamental feature at the top of a wall or arch, or where wall and ceiling meet.

DADO  The lower part of an interior wall, separated from the upper part, or field, by the dado or chair rail.

DENTIL  Ornamental device of small, spaced blocks.

DOG GRATE  A pair of decorative metal stands, or firedogs, used to support logs in an open fire.

*Acanthus leaf*

*Anthemion*

*Palmette*

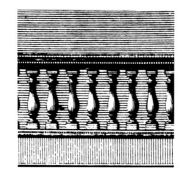

*Balustrade*

*Cartouche*

*Coffering*

DORIC ORDER *see:* Orders. Associated with the mainland temples of Greece. Seen as grand, pure and 'male.'

EGG-AND-DART MOULDING One of the most widely used classical mouldings consisting of egg shapes and 'V' shapes. Originally found in Greek temples, made popular by Palladio.

EMPIRE STYLE A neoclassical style in French interior decoration that reflected Napoleon Bonaparte's ambitions for his new Empire.

ENTABLATURE A horizontal beam connecting a series of columns and forming the upper part of an Order. Divided into cornice (top) frieze (middle) and architrave (bottom).

ETRUSCAN STYLE A style inspired by archaeological researches in the 18th century, characterized by the use of red, black and white with motifs of lions, sphinxes, birds and griffins.

ESCUTCHEON *see:* cartouche.

FANLIGHT A semi-circular window above a door with decorative glazing bars usually radiating out from the centre.

FESTOONS A typically classical Roman ornament of loops of fruit and flowers joined together with ribbons and leaves.

FIELD (of a wall) The upper part between dado and cornice.

FIELDED PANEL A panel raised above its surround.

FILLET A thin, plain moulding, often separating two decorated mouldings.

FINIAL Decorative terminal for pediments, bedposts, etc.

FRET Geometric pattern in which lines meet at right-angles.

FRIEZE A decorative band or strip of decoration. In classical architecture it is the section that lies between the architrave and the cornice.

GOTHIC An ornamental style dating from the 12th century, based on a set of components including the pointed arch, buttresses and vaulting.

GOTHICK An 18th-century passion for picturesque medieval style that had little concern for historical accuracy and is not to be confused with the Gothic revival. Used to give a spurious air of ancient lineage.

GRIFFIN also Griffon. Mythical animal, a mixture between a lion and an eagle, a common motif in heraldry.

HA-HA A sunken fence that divides parkland from garden.

HIPPED ROOF A roof with sloping ends and sides.

IONIC ORDER *see:* Orders. Originating from eastern Greece. A style seen as 'feminine' and slender, used in buildings related to the arts.

JIB DOOR A type of door that visually disappears into the wall treatment.

KEY PATTERN A classical motif of interlocking right-angled and vertical lines, often applied as a continuous pattern.

KEYSTONE Central stone of an arch, often applied as a purely decorative feature.

LAMPIRONS Brackets on the outside of a house to hold lanterns or torches.

LATTICE Diamond-shaped, openwork decoration.

Cornice with frieze above

Corinthian capital

Ionic capital

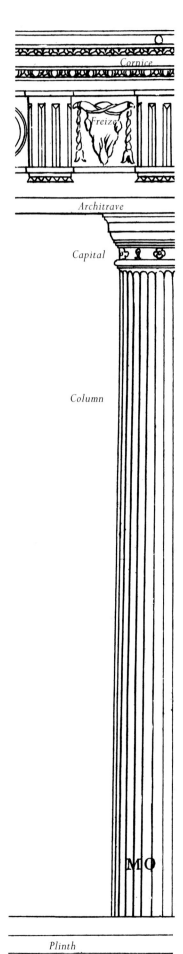

Cornice

Freize

Architrave

Capital

Column

Plinth

MASK  A universal decorative motif representing heads of humans, gods, animals or monsters. Common in ancient Greek and Roman art. Often used as a keystone.

MONOPODIA  A mask-and-animal leg ornament, most often used as a means of support for furniture – on chair and table legs for instance.

NEOCLASSICISM  The mid-18th-century return to Graeco-Roman classicism, as in the Adam style.

ORMULU  Gilded bronze.

OPEN PEDIMENT  A pediment broken at the apex.

ORDERS  The basis of classical architecture. Each Order consists of a column on a pedestal supporting an entablature with a capital. Each order has a different look and purpose – some are tall and decorative, some short and sturdy. *see:* Doric, Ionic, Corinthian, Tuscan and Composite.

PALLADIANISM  The early 18th-century classical revival based on an admiration for the buildings and published works of Andrea Palladio which brought classicism to a wide audience.

PALMETTE  Motif based loosely on a formalized palm leaf. A classical decoration from the Etruscan period.

PANTILE  A roofing tile with an S-shaped cross-section, laid so the downward curve of one tile overlaps the upward curve of its neighbour.

PARAPET WALL  A low wall or railing along the edge of a balcony or roof.

PARLOUR  A room for receiving guests, from the French *parler,* to speak.

PARQUETRY  A geometric pattern of inlaid pieces of wood, usually on a floor.

PATERA  Oval or circular form usually decorated with a formalized flower or rosette.

PEDIMENT  Triangular gable taken from the classical temple, used as an ornament above doors, windows, or on furniture.

PIANO NOBILE  The main floor of a large house containing reception rooms, usually the first floor, from the Italian for grand floor.

PIECRUST  Scrolled, scalloped rim applied mostly to furniture of English origin.

PIER GLASS  A tall, narrow mirror, sometimes one of a pair, designed to hang between windows, usually above a pier table.

PILASTER  Flat, rectangular column form used mainly for decoration rather than support.

PINEAPPLE  Ancient symbol of fertility and, from the late 17th century, of hospitality, hence its use on gate posts, tableware and in guest bedrooms.

PORTICO  Covered entrance to a building.

QUOIN  From the French *coin* for corner. Emphasis given to the corner of a building with alternating long and short horizontal blocks in a contrasting material.

RAILS (of a door)  Horizontal framing member in a door or piece of panelling.

*Festoon*

*Festoon with bucranium and putto*

*Scrolling foliage*

*Key pattern*

*Griffin with finial*

*Fan pattern*

REEDING  Parallel mouldings, the convex equivalent of fluting. Found on fireplace and door surrounds and in furniture design, a decoration frequently used by Thomas Sheraton.

REGENCY  Literally 1811–20, the period when the Prince Regent, later George IV, ruled in place of his father, George III. The decorative style was broadly classical, drawing heavily on the French Empire style.

ROCOCO  A style devised by the French in the early 18th century. A light, airy, frivolous style symptomatic of a relaxing of the formality that pervaded Versailles.

RUSTICATION  Architectural feature consisting of heavy masonry blocks with deep joints, giving a solid feel to the lowest levels of a building.

SALOON  A room in a large house in which guests were received.

SCONCE  A bracket fixed to a wall to hold candles or lights.

SCROLLING FOLIAGE  A decoration consisting of naturalistic forms in abstract, curving lines. Its origins probably lie with the Greek use of the grapevine pattern.

SPHINX  A royal and religious symbol from Ancient Egypt with the body of a lion, the head of a pharaoh (sometimes of a woman) and occasionally wings. In the neoclassical period they supported chair arms and side tables, particularly in Adam-style work.

STRING (of a staircase)  A skirting that covers the ends of the steps in a staircase.

STUCCO  A weather-resistant mixture of lime, powdered marble and glue used as a decorative render on buildings.

SWAG  A pendant garland of fruit or flowers, vegetables, leaves or shells, or a loop of drapery.

TRANSOM  Horizontal member that separates a door from the window above it.

TROMPE L'OEIL  From the French, meaning 'trick the eye'. A painted surface that imitates another or creates an impression of three-dimensional objects.

TUSCAN ORDER  *see:* Orders. The most basic of the Orders, stubby and without ornamentation, associated with simple, rural buildings.

URN  A Greek motif of a lidded vase symbolising death and mourning, both in its emptiness and as an allusion to its more literal function as a receptical for ashes.

VENEER  A thin layer of expensive, often rare wood bonded to common and less expensive base.

VESTIBULE  A small entrance room or anteroom.

VITRUVIAN SCROLL  An undulating wave scroll pattern based on the C-scroll patterns found in classical Greece and Rome.

WAINSCOT  The lower part of the walls of a room, finished in a different material from the upper part.

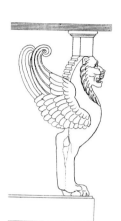

*Monopodia*

*Mask*

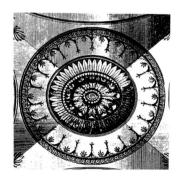

*Patera*

*Corner of a pediment with egg-and-dart moulding.*

*Open pediment with finial*

*Rustication*

# ACKNOWLEDGEMENTS

The author would like to thank her family, friends, clients and all the other house owners who so generously agreed to have their houses photographed and featured in this book.

My thanks also go to the photographer, Kim Sayer for a magnificent job and his patience and commitment to this project. I am also indebted to Collins & Brown for agreeing to take on this book and for transforming the original concept into a stylish finished product – in particular I would like to thank Cindy Richards and Christine Wood.

Lastly, I am grateful to Phillippa Lewis for her research and valuable contacts and my editor, Alexandra Parsons – who once again has produced a great result!

*The publisher would like to thank the following suppliers for providing the materials on pages 182-185*

FIRED EARTH
Twyford Mill Oxford Road Adderbury Oxon OX17 3HP
01295 812 088

COLE & SON
114 Offord Road London N1 1NS
0171 607 3844

# PICTURE CREDITS

All photographs have been taken specially for this book by Kim Sayer, except for the following which appear by kind permission:

The Bridgeman Art Library 14-15, 16-17, 18-19, 20-21, 179, 181
Edifice 12, 34-35, 46, 47, 50, 51, 62
Ianthe Ruthven 8-9, 70, 71, 94-95, 129, 135
Elizabeth Whiting Associates 6-7, 49

# INDEX

Page numbers in *italics* refer to captions